P9-EMD-940
DISCARDED

Perspectives on Partnership — Secondary Initial Teacher Training

Perspectives on Partnership — Secondary Initial Teacher Training

Edited by

Anne Williams

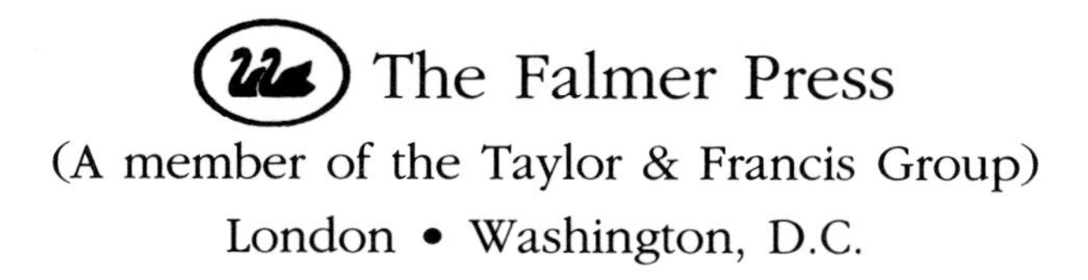

The Falmer Press
(A member of the Taylor & Francis Group)
London • Washington, D.C.

UK The Falmer Press, 4 John Street, London WC1N 2ET
USA The Falmer Press, Taylor & Francis Inc., 1900 Frost Road, Suite 101, Bristol, PA 19007

First published in 1994

A catalogue record for this book is available from the British Library

Library of Congress Cataloging-in-Publication Data are available on request

ISBN 0 7507 0292 3 (cased)
ISBN 0 7507 0293 1 (paper)

Jacket design by Caroline Archer

Typeset in 11/13pt Garamond
Graphicraft Typesetters Ltd., Hong Kong.

Printed in Great Britain by Burgess Science Press, Basingstoke on paper which has a specified pH value on final paper manufacture of not less than 7.5 and is therefore 'acid free'.

Contents

List of Abbreviations

CATE	Council for the Accreditation of Teacher Education
CNAA	Council for National Academic Awards
DES	Department of Education and Science
DFE	Department for Education
FE	Further Education
HEFCE	Higher Education Funding Council for England
HEI	Higher Education Institution
HMI	Her Majesty's Inspectorate
HMSO	Her Majesty's Stationery Office
IAP	Individual Action Planning
INSET	In-service Training
ITE	Initial Teacher Education
LEA	Local Education Authority
LMS	Local Management of Schools
MOTE	Modes of Teacher Education
NCVQ	National Council for Vocational Qualifications
NQT	Newly Qualified Teacher
NVQ	National Vocational Qualification
OHMCI	Office of Her Majesty's Chief Inspector
PGCE	Postgraduate Certificate in Education
QTS	Qualified Teacher Status
SOED	Scottish Office for Education
TEED	Training, Enterprise and Education Directorate
TES	Times Educational Supplement
UFC	Universities Funding Council

Chapter 1

Setting the Scene

Anne Williams

The context for this book is one of a sustained attack upon teacher training in England and Wales which has culminated in proposals for its radical reform (CATE, 1992; Clarke, 1992; DFE, 1992; DFE, 1993). This chapter discusses the context with reference to the content, the location and the control of initial training. It then outlines the contributions to the various perspectives on partnership which are made by the authors of later chapters.

Context

The common features of recent attacks on teacher training in England are that courses are ineffective, that they involve too little time spent in schools working with pupils, and that they contain too much irrelevant theory. Lawlor (1990) expressed the view that the current training system should be abolished on the grounds that the institutions were simply peddling trendy educational theories. Such criticisms have proved difficult if not impossible to counter. Despite the fact that Lawlor has no experience of teaching, that her pamphlet *Teachers Mistaught* (Lawlor, 1990) is based upon information gathered from reading prospectuses and that she has never visited a teacher-training institution, her views have been listened to by successive ministers of state for education. The views of Anthony O'Hear, a philosophy professor, are no better substantiated. Yet in the past year, he has been invited to join CATE (Committee for the Accreditation of Teacher Education) and to add his voice to those who accredit teacher-training courses in this country in spite of his going on record as recommending their abolition (O'Hear, 1988).

The accusation is that control, content and location of teacher-training are all wrong. Content is perceived to be over theoretical, although this would be strongly challenged by many initial training institutions, and there is certainly plenty of evidence of a shift away from theory, especially in postgraduate courses and particularly that which takes the form of the study of the disciplines of education. The location is perceived to be biased heavily in favour of the training institution, rather than the school which is viewed as the most appropriate location for the training of the prospective teacher. Control is seen to be vested far too heavily in the training institutions, despite the influence of the Council for the Accreditation of Teacher Education (CATE), which, since 1984, has had the power to withhold accreditation from courses which fail to meet its requirements. Indeed, training institutions have been accused by Lawlor (1990) of subverting the efforts of CATE and the government and thereby retaining many features of courses which government had intended should disappear.

Current Proposals

The new criteria for the approval of secondary initial teacher training, that is, that dealing with the 11–18 age range, are contained in Circular 9/92 (DFE, 1992). Kenneth Clarke's (then Secretary of State for Education) proposals, when they finally emerged in a consultative document some weeks after his speech to the North of England Education Conference (Clarke, 1992), were that 80 per cent of teacher-training courses should be 'school-based'. This was not defined in the document and had been interpreted by Clarke himself as including work undertaken in higher education institutions but taught by practising teachers. All courses were to meet the new criteria by 1994, not September 1992 as had been reported in the press. In the event, decisions were delayed until after the General Election which was called for April 1992, followed by further delay while a new Secretary of State, John Patten, was appointed.

Ministers claimed that support for the proposals was widespread, and, in principle, this was true. Many institutions had looked enviously at the circumstances which had enabled the Oxford University Department of Educational Studies to resource a course with a high level of teacher involvement on a partnership basis (Benton, 1990). Rather less had been said about the widespread view expressed in responses from schools, as well as from the training institutions, that 80 per cent of the course was too high a proportion to be spent in school and that around 60 per cent was more desirable as well as more realistic. It is reasonably certain that ministers were surprised by the level of resistance to the 80 per cent proposals. Nevertheless, when the criteria were finally published in Circular 9/92, after the delay caused by the General

Election, the new minister chose to over-rule the advice of CATE, which was that twenty-one weeks was realistic and a reasonable compromise, in favour of twenty-four weeks. A further change was a move away from the term 'school-based' to a requirement that the twenty-four weeks should be spent 'physically in schools working with teachers and pupils' (DFE, 1992).

Another significant change in the revised criteria compared with both Circular 3/84 and 24/89 was the shift from a focus upon course content, and counting of hours spent under specified headings, to one which emphasized explicit competences. Much criticism of the earlier criteria had been of the emphasis on guaranteeing that all students spent a specified number of hours upon particular areas of study, regardless of their previous experience or current strengths and weaknesses. This approach seemed mechanistic and inflexible, particularly with respect to postgraduate courses, recruiting ever increasing numbers of mature students with wide-ranging skills and previous experiences, many of them directly related to teaching. For example, guarantees that students spent a specified number of hours upon, for example, information technology related work on targeted topics, despite the fact that some students began the course with skills developed well beyond those offered during the course while others had never used any kind of computer before, manifestly failed to meet the needs of all students.

The final form of the criteria required schools and higher education institutions to work in much closer partnership, with schools taking the lead in significant areas of work, and that schools should be financially rewarded for the additional work which this would entail. Circular 9/92 articulates the principles behind the new proposals as being that:

> 1 schools should play a much larger part in ITT as full partners of higher education institutions (HEIs);
> 2 the accreditation criteria for ITT courses should require HEIs, schools and students to focus on the competencies of teaching; and
> 3 institutions, rather than individual courses, should be accredited for ITT. (DFE, 1992, p. 1)

Subsequent to the publication of Circular 9/92, came an announcement that schools were to be given the opportunity to be funded directly for initial teacher training so that those who so wished could take full responsibility for the training of student teachers, with whatever level of involvement of higher education that they wished and were able to buy in. These courses came under the direct control of the DFE who gave approval and funding. After a year in which a small number of consortia bid successfully for places, a further paper entitled 'The Reform of Initial Teacher Training' was published in September 1993. This proved to have a rather wider remit than the title suggested, as it proposed the setting up of a Teacher Training Agency which would have a planning, accreditation and funding responsibility, but which would fund in-service and research work as well as initial teacher training. While the Minister (John Patten) stated that he expected partnerships between higher education and schools to continue to provide a major route into secondary teaching, he also made clear his intention to increase the level of school-centred provision (DFE, 1993).

Clearly these proposals raise many questions about control, location and content for initial teacher education and each of these three areas is considered below both in relation to each other and in terms of their impact upon the partners in the training process, namely, tutor, teacher and student.

Control of Teacher Education

Prior to the establishment of CATE in 1984, control of the content and process of teacher education was firmly in the hands of the validating body, the university in the case of universities and their affiliated colleges, and the Council for National Academic Awards (CNAA) for other public-sector institutions, largely the polytechnics. In the case of the university, while qualified-teacher status was conferred formally by the Department of Education and Science on the recommendation of the institution, the university effectively controlled the course and the award of the qualification. The government controlled numbers, and had increased control over teacher supply through giving subject-specific targets rather than overall targets for initial teacher training students and also by shifting emphasis from the four-year BEd route to the one-year postgraduate certificate route, thereby enabling change in teacher numbers to be effected relatively quickly.

CATE took the first steps towards reducing the control exercised by the higher education institutions (HEIs) by establishing criteria which all courses had to meet in order to be accredited to train teachers, although some flexibility was possible in interpreting and implementing some requirements. Circular 3/84 was replaced by Circular 24/89 which increased the level of prescription. Given the interventionist approach of government over the past decade to many aspects of education, it is no surprise to see teacher education receiving the same treatment. What is perhaps less expected is to see control being increasingly given to the very teaching force which has been so pilloried by successive ministers of education, for failing to maintain or to raise standards in schools. Thus, control of initial teacher training, on the one hand, has come under increasing control from central government, which, having set up CATE as a non-elected body, with its members selected by the Secretary of State, has made an increasing number of political appointments to its main committee and has reduced the proportion of 'education professionals' on the committee. At the same time, control also has been taken from Higher Education Institutions through the requirement of Circular 9/92 that schools and teachers should become full partners in the training process and should be involved fully in all aspects of the course. Subsequent invitations to school consortia to bid for school-centred courses, removes completely control of some initial teacher-training courses from higher education.

The Location of Teacher Education

Location in relation to teacher education can be interpreted in different ways. Prior to the drafting of new accreditation documentation, considerable attention had been given to approaches to initial teacher education seen to be 'school-based'. Various patterns already existed. Oxford University received considerable publicity and public acclaim from ministers and representatives of the Department for Education for its course in which students, called 'interns', spent a significant amount of time in school, working with both tutors and teachers. Sussex University has run for some twenty-five years a 'school-based' course in which students spend three days a week in school throughout their course. A new initiative, the Articled Teacher Scheme, involved participants in a two-year course, four-fifths of which was spent in school. Significantly, this latter course had proved to be considerably more expensive than the conventional Postgraduate Certificate in Education Course (£10,000 per student compared with £6,000 in 1991/1992 outside London), and the 1992 cohort was the last to train for secondary teaching by this route.

The location of training can refer to two things. It can be used simply as a measure of the amount of time spent in schools. It also can be used to indicate a level of involvement and responsibility on the part of partner teachers in the schools which is above the pre-Circular 9/92 norm. It is with regard to the latter interpretation that courses such as those offered by Oxford and Sussex, and also those which prepare Articled Teachers, differ from most others. Many institutions are able to claim that courses are school-based in terms of the amount of time that students spend in school. Far fewer can claim a high level of teacher involvement over and above the supervision of teaching practice. This is, in many instances, a matter of resourcing rather than a matter of choice.

Related to time given to school-based work is the issue of the extent to which schools are to be 'in the lead'. This raises the issue of the relationship between location and control. In the recent past, a number of courses have been located substantially in school but controlled entirely by the Higher Education Institution, subject to the constraints of CATE. The new criteria mention a number of specific areas (teaching of specialist subjects, assessment of pupils, management of classes, supervision of students, assessing their competence) in which schools are to be in the lead, prompting some institutions to comment that they might not be prepared to continue to validate a course for which they appeared to have so little control. Others have taken the view that it is possible to argue that schools always have had a leading impact in these areas because students spend a major part of their course in schools which therefore have to have a significant influence upon them. Following this argument, it can be claimed that the articulation of this in the Circular is largely an endorsement of an existing state of affairs. A reply from the Department for Education to a query from the head of one of the country's largest university departments of education, that a leading responsibility does not imply exclusive responsibility, suggests that such an argument is tenable. Nevertheless, for many institutions, the change in both location and control will be a significant one, even though a minimum of fifteen weeks have to be spent in schools under the 24/89 criteria (DES, 1989).

The Content of Teacher Education

Criticism of initial teacher training has centred upon the perceived excesses of theory which are supposedly offered by training institutions. Both the fact that so much theory as opposed to practice is included in courses and the nature of that theory, which is described as trendy and irrelevant, have come under attack. Earlier CATE criteria (DES, 1984, 1989) had addressed course content by specifying time to be spent on certain aspects, (e.g., that undergraduate courses should contain at least two years of 'subject study'), or requiring their inclusion, (e.g., that there should be separate institution-based courses addressing classroom management), or specifying what students should be taught, (e.g., how to avoid preconceptions based on race or gender).

Circular 9/92 continues the trend which first appeared in Circular 24/89 by shifting emphasis from course content to the competences needed by the newly qualified teacher. These are described under five headings: subject knowledge; subject application; classroom management; assessment and recording progress; further professional development.

Interest in the idea of competence-based teacher education is not new, although there has been much resistance to the approach in England, based partly upon the reductionism which appears to have accompanied moves in this direction in the USA and partly upon concerns about a perceived conflict between competence-based approaches and reflective teaching. Preliminary results from an Economic and Social Science Research Council funded project into initial teacher education suggest that a minority of courses (10 per cent of undergraduate and primary, 3 per cent of secondary and postgraduate) subscribe to what they describe as a 'competency model' of a teacher, with the overwhelming majority of courses describing their agreed model of a teacher as that of reflective practitioner (Barrett *et al.*, 1992).

Moves in the direction of the use of competences are evident in Circular 24/89 which specifies exit criteria for certain elements of initial teacher training. For example, ITT courses should develop in student teachers,

> . . . a breadth and depth of subject knowledge extending beyond the demands of programmes of study or examination syllabuses in schools (Cr 4.5iii).
> . . . the capacity to use a range of teaching methods appropriate to the different abilities and other needs of pupils and organise their work accordingly (Cr 6.3iii). (DES, 1989, pp. 8 and 10)

This follows the circulation to Local Education Authorities in 1989 of exit criteria for Licensed Teachers, such as the requirement that Licensed Teachers should have competence in delivery of subjects they are required to teach.

In 1991 the National Curriculum Council articulated the needs of newly qualified teachers with respect to the National Curriculum in terms of exit competences, such as:

- to understand the different purposes of assessment (formative, diagnostic, summative, and evaluative); and

- to understand the nature of National Curriculum assessment which combines teachers' assessment with statutory or non-statutory assessment tasks.

Circular 9/92 thus builds upon earlier steps in the direction of competences while extending their application significantly. In also stating that these competences are not expected to constitute the whole of an initial training course, the Circular avoids one of the difficulties which is associated with competence-based approaches. This is the problem of reconciling performance in terms of identified competences with overall 'competence'. That is, it is possible to get a tick for every part of a list of individual competences but still be deemed incompetent in the classroom.

The wording of the competences in Circular 9/92 also offers some reassurance to those who fear the reductionist approach of some earlier competence models and who see a conflict between competence-based models and those based upon reflective practice. Where competences are expressed in broad terms there seems no reason why they should not be used in conjunction with the development of reflective practice, particularly when used in conjunction with profiling, also currently appearing in Initial Teacher Training courses, and demanding reflection and self-evaluation on the part of the student teacher. It is also argued, for example by Hextall *et al.* (1991), that the quality of reflectivity can be formulated as competences that can be monitored.

Partnerships in Practice

This book brings together accounts of different approaches to, and perspectives upon, aspects of partnership. To put subsequent chapters into a context, Peter Lucas offers a timely reminder of what it is that still draws young people into teaching, through his account of what teachers, at an early stage in their careers, found rewarding. Some of the examples he gives could refocus our thinking about how the experience of the student teacher is structured. For example, is sufficient attention given to the benefits which can accrue from teaching several parallel groups? Others hint at the kinds of experiences which could be as fulfilling for the student teacher as for the newly-qualified teacher (NQT), such as the opportunity to take pupils away for a residential experience. Some students have this experience now: the enthusiasm with which the NQT quoted here talks of that opportunity might give those of us who may be reassessing the value of that activity for our own students, pause for thought.

Given the support for the competence-based approach which currently emanates from the DFE and from ministers, Geoff Whitty's analysis of what competences are or might be offers reassurance about the present structure together with a warning of possible pitfalls. He goes on to describe how a Northern Ireland working group addressed the challenge of defining the competences expected of a successful professional teacher, and then prioritizing them in the context of initial teacher training, induction and further professional development, of using them in practice and of assessing them.

The chapters which follow all give accounts of how partnerships have been set up in three very different contexts. While clear differences in both the approach adopted and the processes which have been needed to set up the three schemes, all illustrate the importance of time and the need to build a partnership structure over a number of years. Leicester based their ITT work upon an ITT/INSET model which recognized the potential benefits for both students and teachers, whether the latter be school- or higher education-based. Courses were developed which, while making the student the main focus, also enabled the other partners to benefit. Developments post 9/92 have thus been able to build upon a longstanding partnership model. Oxford's course developed with a great deal of support, financial and otherwise, from the LEA who considered that the funding of schools to be involved in ITT was worthwhile because of the staff development benefits which could accrue and for the advantages for it in terms of teacher recruitment. Goldsmiths, working in a very different context, where there is considerable competition between the various higher education providers of initial teacher training, have built upon a successful initiative developed by one subject area over many years.

Having looked, at an institutional level, at what partnership means for three universities, the remaining chapters consider partnership from the perspective of several of the partners involved, the student, the headteacher, the higher education tutor and the school mentor. Student views are based upon a study of students from four different initial teacher-training institutions who were interviewed at the end of their PGCE year, and suggest that good quality higher education support is seen by them as both relevant and beneficial during both institution and school-based parts of a course. Their views do, however, raise questions about the value of higher education support unless high quality can be guaranteed. Barbara Wynn gives an account of the factors which the school head, as manager of the school side of the partnership, has to consider and reminds us that there are both costs and benefits to schools who choose to involve themselves in this work. Graham Butt gives a view of the higher education tutor's role in a partnership course and argues for a continued distinctive contribution from higher education. The perspective of the mentor is given through a discussion of possible approaches to mentoring in initial teacher training, followed by an account of issues raised by mentors during the early days of the development of a partnership course.

The kinds of partnerships which are currently being developed by providers of secondary initial teacher training are in their infancy and many issues remain to be resolved. There is still scope for variation in the level of school involvement, from total responsibility within a school-centred scheme, to what is still a limited commitment from schools which are satellites to partnership schemes which have chosen to involve a proportion of schools in detailed planning teaching and review while offering more limited involvement to others. The extent to which schools are prepared or able to commit themselves to greatly increased inputs to the initial training process remains uncertain. At the time of writing, Harrow school has chosen to terminate its involvement with a partnership scheme, claiming that its senior staff cannot afford to spend the time supervising five trainees (TES, 1994). The reporter notes that if a school as well resourced as Harrow feels unable to contribute without diverting attention from its main priority which must be its pupils, what chance for those less fortunate?

Equally uncertain is the number of schools interested in taking full responsibility for training students or the level of financial incentive which will be offered to tempt them down this road. The contributors to this book, both authors of particular chapters and the students and mentors who have given their views, support future partnerships which involve schools and higher education. It is their hope that ways will be found to make best possible use of the potential contribution of both.

References

Barrett, E., Barton, L., Furling, J., Galvin, C., Miles, S. and Whitty, C. (1993) *Initial Teacher Education in England and Wales: A Topography*, London, University of London, Goldsmiths College.

Benton, P. (1990) (Ed) *The Oxford Internship Scheme*, London, Calouste Gulbenkian Foundation.

CATE (Committee for the Accreditation of Teacher Education) (1992) *The Accreditation of Initial Teacher Training under Circulars 9/92 (Department For Education) and 35/92 (Welsh Office)*, A note of guidance from the Council for the Accreditation of Teachers, London, CATE.

CLARKE, K. (1992) 'Speech presented to North of England Education Conference', 4 January.

DES (Department of Education and Science) (1984) *Initial Teacher Training: Approval of Courses (Circular 3/84)*, London, HMSO.

DES (Department of Education and Science) (1989) *Initial Teacher Training: Approval of Courses (Circular 24/89)*, London, HMSO.

DES (Department of Education and Science)/HMI (Her Majesty's Inspectorate) (1991) *School-based Initial Training in England and Wales*, London, HMSO.

DFE (Department For Education) (1992) *Initial Teacher Training: (Secondary Phase) (Circular 9/92)*, London, HMSO.

DFE (Department For Education) (1993) *The Reform of Initial Teacher Training*, London, HMSO.

HEXTALL, I., LAWN, M., MENTER, L., SIDGWICK, S. and WALKER, S. (1991) *Imaginative Projects: Arguments for a New Teacher Education*, London, Goldsmiths College.

LAWLOR, S. (1990) *Teachers Mistaught: Training in Theories or Education in Subjects*, London, Centre for Policy Studies.

NCC (National Curriculum Council) (1991) *The National Curriculum and the Initial Training of Student, Articled and Licensed Teachers*, York, NCC.

O'HEAR, A. (1988) *Who Teaches the Teachers?*, London, Social Affairs Unit. *Times Educational Supplement* (1994), 11 February p. 3.

Chapter 2

The Pleasures of Teaching

Peter Lucas

> I've done different jobs before . . . teaching. One of the major highlights is actually just liking the job overall. (Teacher in 1st post-PGCE year)

> Numerous. Where do I begin? There are so many, I'm just trying to picture one. (Teacher in 5th post-PGCE year)

That teaching can be a wonderfully satisfying job can tend to be insufficiently attended to in discussions about, and analyses of initial teacher (ITE) and the induction of newly qualified teachers (NQTs). If it isn't the traditional vocabulary of the old ITE paradigm — the talk of 'culture shocks' and 'baptisms of fire', of 'ivory towers' and the 'real world' of classrooms — then it's concern over the parameters of the new one: the respective roles of university teachers and school mentors, their concerns and fears and aspirations, the precise nature of mentoring, the quality of the institutional partnership between university and school, the implications for staffing (in schools and universities) of the new funding arrangements, the possibilities for school consortia who may or may not decide to 'go it alone' without benefit of higher education, the extent to which ITE has security of tenure within universities, and the tension between the concepts and practices of 'training' and 'education'. In the increasing torrent of words spent on these issues, the joys of working with pupils don't seem to get much of a mention, and yet they are central to the job. Accordingly this contribution seeks to remind us of them by narrating the perceptions of NQTs and others rather more experienced. In celebrating such perceived highlights, it also analyses a selection of them to try to understand the implications they may have for the preparation of student teachers and the induction of beginners.

The data is drawn from an enquiry, begun in 1992, into the relationship between the notions of 'reflective practice' and the 'socialization of' of new teachers. Twenty-five teachers who had been on the same secondary PGCE programme in an English university between 1985 and 1992 were interviewed[1]. All were specialists in the same subject. The subject application course they followed was set within an overall PGCE programme the rhetoric of which embraced the concept of reflective practice (as systematic enquiry into one's own subject) and was intended to offer a coherent and practical expression of it. Nearly all of the teachers in the study were teaching in state comprehensive schools in different parts of the country.

Each teacher was interviewed at length, using a semi-structured schedule, the focuses of which included perceived highlights in his or her career up to that point. The questions were not made known in detail in advance of the interviews in order to preserve spontaneity of response. The interviews (with one exception) were audio-recorded (with the agreement of the interviewee) and transcripts made; notes were also made at the time by the interviewer. Selection of the interviewees was largely, but not exclusively, determined by tutors' estimates of the quality of their reflectivity as student teachers during their ITE year.

Beginners is not a completely satisfactory term. Riseborough and Poppleton (1991) use it for those in their first five years of teaching. However, some teachers may achieve quite quickly forms of 'maturity' expressed in high and assured levels of skill and understanding whilst others may have to be more persistent. Here, for convenience, the term refers to those in their first six years because the more experienced ones are looking back over their earlier professional years. The year of teaching is indicated in brackets. Approximately one third of the study teachers were between twenty-eight and thirty-five, and a similar fraction were women. Letters are used to preserve teachers' anonymity.

What They Said

An examination of the teachers' responses reveals, very quickly, a range of highlights, touching upon a considerable variety of issues. They include: actually surviving the first year and realizing that one could do the job as a full-time member of staff; feeling an accepted part of the school community; taking pleasure in, and drawing confidence and insights from the enthusiasm and competence of particular colleagues; having good relationships with pupils, evidenced for example by being the recipient of a pupil's trust or cheery greetings in the corridor; getting to know pupils better away from the classroom on residential courses; helping them achieve sporting successes; guiding form pupils successfully through the five years of their compulsory secondary schooling; learning that their pupils have succeeded in external examinations and that they (the teachers) 'haven't let them down'; recognizing developing competence; observing their pupils' understanding occur; observing their faces as they enjoy challenging outdoor experiences; beginning consciously (and with success) to stretch the range of their teaching strategies by going beyond tried, tested and 'safe' methods; realizing that the decisions they have stood by, not without risk, have been vindicated; learning to become increasingly skilled in the manœuvrings of collaborative curriculum innovation; becoming aware of how their understanding of the nature of teaching has become much deeper than hitherto; receiving praise from pupils, from colleagues, from visiting teachers, and from parents; having the written evidence of pupils' comments and choices confirming that they have helped to improve the standing of their department in the eyes of the pupils and the school; developing as effectively as possible cross-phase links; gaining promotion; and having the satisfaction whilst recognizing the awesomeness of being a particular pupil's acknowledged role model.

Such highlights were a source of great pleasure to these teachers. There are no surprises here. These are the sorts of things we would expect. But such a list is a powerful reminder of the attractions of the job and, more importantly here, an inducement to explore further the teachers' perceptions. The quotations which follow give an indication of what the perceived successes meant to individuals. By quoting the teachers' words in this way, without in this section commenting on particular ones, I am able to draw on their expressiveness and at the same time, 'to signal respect for (them) . . . by allowing others . . . to hear their voices in print' (Ruddock, 1993, p. 19). Moreover, in so doing I can also underline the fact that 'the educational system of a country is kept in place and kept running by the actions and efforts of thousands of people, all of whom are devoting a considerable part of their lives to it. They find that their own lives are changed by the efforts they are making. Each of their individual selves change and are changed by both small and large scale educational developments' (Griffiths, 1993, p. 151). Such considerations are in keeping with the tone and nature of this chapter.

> One of the best decisions I made was to take the tutor group . . . someone was ill . . . and they asked me if I would consider. So I said 'Yes', against the better advice of others, and although

it's constant grief, I'm really glad I've got it now, I've really enjoyed that. I think it's brought me into the school. (G, 1)

I'm not being conceited but I certainly feel that I have a better relationship with all the kids I know than the vast majority of the staff who've been there for a long time. I mean they have remarked on it . . . and it's great for me to walk down the corridor, and even kids I don't teach, they say, 'Oh hello, Mr . . .', and I think, 'Who are you?' But they all obviously know that you're approachable, and I love it. (B, 1)

I suppose the biggest highlight has got to be the promotion (to Co-ordinator of Lower School Humanities) . . . being recognized by the school for what we've been doing, and there's been lots of moments through the two years where things have happened . . . the new modules . . . we've got . . . one of the best ones. The first battle we had within the Faculty was about getting a marking scheme . . . policy would be a better phrase . . . and then an assessment policy which followed. The idea of integration actually happening rather than . . . geography and history being two distinct subject areas. (S, 2)

Something that I've become particularly involved with this year has been with junior school liaison . . . we have an open catchment area here. It's a delicate area because of that, . . . four secondary schools competing for about seventeen feeder schools . . . I've . . . worked with teachers in various primary schools trying to build up decent schemes that work . . . it's given me a personal insight into the pupils . . . in an earlier stage of development . . . that's been particularly interesting. (U, 2)

. . . we wrote . . . a flexible study unit on the Aztecs before the final (National Curriculum History) document came out, which was a bit stupid of us, but we did it and we thought, 'Well, we'll try that anyway'. So we did that and that was brilliant. I really loved doing that . . . We've translated it for the primary school, our feeder schools, so now I go into two feeder schools one lesson a week and support them doing it. I've enjoyed doing that. (W, 2)

. . . when I started I had a bottom set fourth-year class, on a Tuesday afternoon and a Friday afternoon. I mean that wasn't a highlight at all for a start because that was really hard work, but by the end of the two years, I really enjoyed teaching that class, and we were sort of working together. I think that was a highlight and an encouragement and a boost . . . (M, 3)

. . . when it's the final lesson (that year of three separate fifth-year classes) and at the end . . . they come up to you and shake your hand and say, 'Cor, it's been a pleasure, sir, it's been a really good two years.' And although they don't all do that by any means, the three or four that do it and say [they] 'really enjoyed the two years, it's been brilliant', I think is a tremendous feeling, and that to me is something that makes the job worthwhile on its own. (P, 3)

I think rather than any one particular incident or event, . . . just the . . . way that between us we've managed to turn the department round . . . I think it is very strong at the moment, . . . I've just been filling in first and second-year profiles and reading the pupils' comments on them, all very positive comments. (D, 3)

. . . getting them [form pupils] through the five years . . . I'd call that a highlight because a lot of them had problems when they first started, and all of them except one managed to finish the fifth year . . . I learnt a lot from them. I developed quite a lot on the pastoral side. (T, 5)

Last year I ran a trip, an adventure trip down to Spain, and seeing the kids on that, that was fantastic. Just watching them, we were doing some water-skiing and watching them pop out of the water, and when they pop out of the water they're sort of cheering, you know, you can see, just the reaction on their faces. It's moments like that, more than anything, they're the highlights, and . . . how you can see a smile on a face when they actually succeed in doing something in the classroom. I've got a couple of kids in the form who are quite weak in many areas but if you can just sit down and persevere with them eventually they can see the light and there's a smile which appears on their face. things like that. These are the highlights . . . it happens all the time. (X, 5)

. . . I think a highlight of anybody's career is enjoying the people you work with and maintaining a sense of humour and sense of building friendship. (E, 5)

> Planning — wondering if it will work — and it works! Being on the edge of things. (C, 6)

> . . . developing coursework has always been what I regard as [an] exceptionally brilliant and enjoyable [aspect of teaching] and so when I'm doing that, and then I put it into practice, I'm at my happiest. (Y, 6)

What can we learn from such perceived highlights about the conditions of learning to be a teacher? What can we learn that may help us prepare student teachers and induct beginners more wisely? To answer these questions I want to examine these aspects much more closely: the allocation of classes, the relationship between collaboration and individuality, the role of key colleagues, and the place of residentials.

The Significance of Parallel Encounters

It may be that we do not attach sufficient importance to giving beginners the opportunity to teach the same topics to at least two, possibly more, classes in the same year. Looking back over his first five years, E, 5 claimed that 'one of the great' experiences, the most satisfying periods, that stood out, arose from the number of first-year classes he had been given when he first arrived at his school: five out of a total of seven groups. He had to make his own resources for the most part, but he had 'had lots of exciting ideas'. Having to be inventive in this context had been 'very exciting', and ultimately (although, of course he didn't know it at the time) there was to be a very satisfying pay-off. His teaching of those pupils continued into their second and third years; so, too, did his inventions and preparation of resources. When the pupils got to the third year they had to select a humanities subject.

> . . . and they opted for history . . . that's when we had the largest uptake — 140. I feel that I'd been largely responsible for making history an exciting and rewarding option within the school. I was very excited about that.

Although he now felt that to have five such classes was really too many for a beginner, because it had made his experience in that first year rather too compacted and limited, 'to get two or three classes that are similar in the school year can be important in terms of reflection . . .' He, himself, had gained. The opportunity to compare the responses of classes had been 'advantageous to my reflective skills'. Other teachers felt they too had benefited from this kind of experience. B, 1 had been given three Y7 and four Y9 classes. When he had first seen his timetable, he remembered thinking, 'I don't fancy this', and reckoning that his teaching was too heavily weighted towards the younger pupils. But, by the time of the interview, held in the third term of his first year, he was strongly aware that having so many younger classes had 'been good for' him. His explanation was linked to his perception of the nature of his PGCE subject application course. These parallel classes were,

> following the same syllabus, but I'd tinker a little bit with the lesson every time, sometimes drastically if it hasn't gone well. And if it's gone really well, I'll still tinker and try something a little bit different, and you try and gauge from how it's received . . . their end product, their thoughts and work on it, . . . and discipline, . . . if it's a buzz . . . and you know it's all to do with the work you think it's been well received, but if it's a distracted talking about last night's football or something else which has not necessarily to do with the nature of the lesson you know that perhaps something has . . . gone wrong and they're not as . . . focused as they could be . . . I tend to gauge it for factors like that . . . I find it quite useful to have those similar classes at different points in the week because then you can tinker with it . . . I'll sort of do a lesson plan for the first thing on the Monday and I'll have the same lesson last thing on a Monday and I'll know I'll teach it differently even before I've done the first lesson.

The opportunity provided by parallel classes had in a sense transformed the classrooms into laboratories. Ideas could be tried out and evaluated as was done during the PGCE year so there was a fruitful continuity of experience. With 'the way [his PGCE subject] was set up', B, 1 commented, his experience during his first year of teaching 'was a continuation of the course because you're still practising'. In other words, this particular timetabled context set up a structure which protected and stimulated any disposition to reflect. After a lesson early in the week he would immediately think,

> I didn't like the way that went, I didn't feel comfortable doing that, What am I going to do for the last lesson?

and 'I can change it.'

Coming to the end of his third year of teaching, and in his second school, D, 3 believed that he was 'quite fortunate at the moment in that I've got four first-year classes and three second-year classes.' He could take note of reactions. Like B, 1, he was deliberately experimental, in the interests of his own enjoyment and also of pupils' interest. 'I try not to have the same two lessons.' He was also alert to taken-for-granted assumptions, e.g., about vocabulary, which were sharply exposed in this 'parallel class' situation.

These brief accounts point up the following features that are worth noting in any consideration of where a teacher might be in terms of his or her professional development. First, a commitment to experimentation beyond the achievement of 'success' (even if the lesson had 'gone really well', I try not to have the same lesson twice); second, recognition of the need to overcome the imprisoning quality of 'everyday assumptions'; third, an attention to different types of evidence (pupils' 'end product', their 'thoughts', the 'discipline' required, the contrast between a 'healthy buzz' and 'distracted talking'); fourth, a cumulative satisfaction from regularly and customarily examining the effectiveness of their teaching; and fifth, an attachment to a specific style of enquiry into their work — the comparative — which looks as if it encourages 'living-in-the-question' (Pascale, 1990, citing Erhard 1984), surely a desirable condition of learning, and not just for beginners.

Quite clearly, the perceptions of these teachers of the impact of timetable allocations on their professional development invite school staff responsible for such decisions to reconsider the conditions in which their beginners are being placed — and to reconsider also the underlying rationale. Some timetablers and heads of department may say, 'Well, we do this sort of thing already.' But, if this is the case, do they also investigate the reasons for doing so? From the perspective of 'micropolitics' — defined as 'consist(ing) of the strategies by which individuals and groups in organisational contexts seek to use their resources of authority and influence to further their interests' (Hoyle, 1986, p. 126) — a perspective actually taken by one of this study's teachers viewing the school as a whole, the younger classes may be 'foisted' upon the younger and/or less experienced members of staff. Suggested factors behind such perceived compulsion included concern that the latter wouldn't be able to deal effectively with examination classes, a preference on the part of the experienced teachers for older pupils because those teachers were not used to actually dealing with the younger ones (a lot of staff didn't want them), and uncertainty about National Curriculum attainment targets, which led to older staff seeking advice from those colleagues who, although younger and less experienced, were possibly more knowledgeable because of their recent initial training.

If we seek to enhance the conditions of learning of beginners (and, indeed, for student teachers and teachers with considerable experience) a parallel-classes environment can cut time spent on preparation, thus making more time available for reflection on how to make one's teaching more effective. Differences between similar classes in the reception of similar approaches and materials helps to promote re-thinking and creates appropriate conditions for enquiries into one's teaching, even if initially such enquiries might take more primitive and imperfect forms than action research purists would prefer. Note that more than 'tinkering' may take place.

Collaboration and Individuality

Traditionally, teachers are seen as working in isolation, their time-shared classrooms symbolic of a confining individualism. The benefits to teachers of undermining such 'privatism' and developing collaboration have been strongly and persuasively urged. Indeed, in various ways (mentoring schemes in ITE and the challenges of the National Curriculum, for example) the education system has been propelling teachers, and continues to propel them towards more cooperative effort. However, collaboration often takes place in ways that do not impact fundamentally on individuals' attitudes or practices. On the other hand, if they do impact, or if collegiality is overplayed and becomes politically correct, individuality may suffer. Two accounts, those of I, 3 and J, 1 seem to me to be particularly illuminative of a crucial aspect of the relationship between the teacher as lonely professional (the traditional paradigm) and the teacher as collaborator, and one of which we must be careful to take account.

I, 3's 'pinnacle', as he referred to it, 'at the moment', was a visit to France, 'a joint venture between modern languages, history and drama', focusing on the Normandy Landings and the story of twins who, having been apart, met once more on the beach: 'a drama with historical content'. The large degree of responsibility given to the pupils with regard to organization — raising money, the ferry, accommodation — was matched by their responsibility for 'shaping' the drama 'and researching the history'. In these ways their school's philosophy regarding student responsibility was actualized. The beaches and the museum were visited, and 'we actually performed the drama in several schools in France'. Here, three departments got together on a significant and challenging enterprise, going well beyond the everyday experience of the classroom: it was 'joint work', not just between colleagues but with pupils as well. The impact on I, 3 himself, was considerable.

> I just learned so much about myself and teaching from that experience . . . those kids who went on that trip with me are . . . just feel very close . . . I really . . . understood what it meant to be a teacher . . . It fired up for me history again, occasionally you need that . . . it really sank in that this is an incredibly important subject . . . we cannot let it disappear, we cannot let it become something trivialized . . . it's . . . about people and feelings and how people thought and reasons for it . . . at the beginning, the kids would say, 'What's this? . . . What does this mean?', and I'd search around and say, 'Well, what about trying this?' . . . by the end the same students were actually trying to work it out themselves. So it gave me a real insight into seeing what it means to actually be a partnership with your students rather than this all-knowing teacher, which I really, I doubted it existed . . . (I, 3)

Clearly, I, 3 is reporting on what Maslow has termed a 'peak experience', a 'profound learning experience', containing 'moments of revelation, of illumination, insight, understanding, ecstasy'. (Maslow, 1978, p. 171) The collaboration in which he took part seems to have had the effect of enhancing his 'individuality' through his refocusing on the meaning of what he was doing as a teacher.

J, 1 felt herself to be in a supportive department and it is appropriate to identify some features. Her head of history's 'door is always open'. If she'd had a lesson she was concerned about, 'he'd tell me, well you know, think about why it went wrong, and how next lesson I can get up again . . . I am always able to talk to him about it . . .' The head of her other subject was also accessible and aided her. She clearly felt able to talk freely with her colleagues: 'I can do the job because I have the support of the people around me.' She had observed colleagues teach, the head of history with a Y9 class, 'and I've seen through the [field] trip the ways that members of the geography department teach', although it is clear she would have liked more observational opportunities. 'Unfortunately, there's not a lot of time in which to do it . . . I haven't done it nearly as much as I'd like to, basically.' There had been a paired lesson with an A-level colleague, and 'a couple of instances' with a colleague in geography. The previous afternoon she and the

A-level colleague had been planning together for future work: 'what we're trying to achieve, what we've got to do, and topics and resources, so there's always a chance to talk.' She was jointly endeavouring to set up a history field trip to be held later that term. Within the school there was a 'probationer support group which meets three or four times a year'.

She rated her colleagues as 'very important' in terms of making her question what she was doing and to try something new. Her history colleagues' style of observation of her lessons she perceived as similar to the 'partnership supervision' exercised by her tutor during her teaching practices, and she herself looked forward to using such a style with a student teacher beginning the following year, although she intended to begin with a team teaching approach. She referred to a lesson after which she 'found [it] quite amazing' when the head of history said he could learn from 'the way I . . . picked up on everything that was going on around me — what's it called? — 'withitness', I think.' Another history colleague at the end of a lesson had said, 'Can I keep this lesson? Can I take it away with me? Can I keep your class?'

The specific lesson under consideration here was, briefly, evidence-based, incorporative of pupil research and role-play and designed to stimulate reasoning. According to J, 1, it was mostly the brain-child of a colleague, but not exclusively so — 'a collaboration of ideas from lots of people' had occurred, she said. Moreover, she recalled that prior to the lesson, she had, at home, systematically and carefully thought through step by step how she was going to introduce the work to the class, a top set. The lesson was observed by three primary-school liaison teachers, there with a view to sending children to her school, and representing one of the 'external publics' (Williams, 1989, p. 19) with whom secondary teachers increasingly find themselves crucially involved. J, 1 reported that afterwards they'd told her they'd really enjoyed it, and that it was a pleasure to have been there. Her own conclusion was that 'it was a really good lesson; we had a lot of fun; the end result was quite spectacular.' In analysing what she had got out of it, J, 1 put it into perspective and recalled how she had noticed over the two years, the training years and this year, that her power both to explain and to give instructions had improved.

In the case of J, 1, there had been a particular challenge because of the complexity of what she had to explain to the pupils to enable the lesson to succeed. What had struck her was the quality and quantity of her pupils' thinking: . . . 'the ideas they were coming out with, they were quite amazing . . . high-powered thinking . . . and it was just so nice to think that something that I had explained and initiated could result in such a major thought process, and everyone was so actively involved.' And there was the added satisfaction, of course, of having her expertise, which she felt was continuing to grow, observed and confirmed by the primary colleagues present. The lesson, which itself emphasized pupils cooperating with one another, was mainly one colleague's idea, but J, 1, by her own thorough engagement with it, had surely put her own stamp on it. Her role in that collaborative departmental setting enhanced her individuality: she felt that she had moved forward as a teacher.

A recent, powerful and accessible case for what they call 'interactive professionalism' has been put by Fullan and Hargreaves (1992). Their case is the more persuasive because they acknowledge the very real dangers of collegiality (e.g., 'groupthink') and are careful to give emphasis to the role of the individual. This is not the place for a comprehensive analysis of the pros and cons of collaboration and individualism, but it is the place to pose a question for those responsible for the school-based preparation of student teachers and the induction of beginners. The question arises from the two accounts narrated above within the context of the relationship between being collaborative and being an individual. How are you ensuring that collaboration honestly deserving the description 'jointwork' (Little, 1990) takes place in a form and setting perceived by student teachers and beginners (and capable of being persuasively and evidentially described by them) as 'self-actualizing'? Fullan and Hargreaves rightly say that it is important to remember that 'if we seek to eliminate *individualism* (habitual patterns of working alone), we should eradicate *individuality* (voicing of disagreement, opportunity for solitude, and *experiences of personal meaning*) with' (p. 59. The last emphasis is mine).

Key Colleagues

Key sources of development for beginners are 'significant others' among their colleagues. For Z, 1, she was someone with whom he talked a lot, who was constantly evaluating her teaching, and who 'seems to be completely dedicated 100 per cent at all times'. Like others she was a teacher of a subject not his own in the humanities area. Z, 1 was aware of aspects that he perceived as problematic, but was 'sure [that] having this person, . . . within the same working area, is a very positive influence on me.' N, 1, strongly concerned not to fail his slow learners, felt that he had learnt a lot observing the style of a support teacher working with one pupil in his own classroom: he had been, he said, very fortunate to have such opportunities. His technology and geography colleagues had impressed him: 'they've been teaching a while but their methods are certainly not out of place . . . they're very thoughtful.' D, 3 and his head of department 'sort things out as we're going along, and it's a really good working atmosphere and relationship.' Between them they had 'managed to turn the [history] department round', and for this conclusion he had the evidence of pupil comments.

M, 3 referred to a colleague who was excellent at giving help and advice when she became a sixth-form tutor. '. . . Instead of saying well this is how you do it . . . he would talk you through what was going through your mind rather than just saying . . . 'this is all you need to do, just give them this and say that.' He would actually try to find out what exactly it was you were having problems with . . . he was getting you to actually talk through it yourself and come out with your own ideas basically.' At her second school, F, 5 had worked with an excellent historian and an excellent teacher. This gave her the opportunity of 'working with someone who was . . . an expert in his area, the use of sources, especially. He got me much more into that. He was also very much into language, and so he made me think a lot about the language we use in the classroom.' It was at that school, where the pupils were much more responsive and she didn't have to be the tough disciplinarian, that she was able to become (using her words) a real teacher. E, 5 contrasted the collaborative ethos on his subject application course — which he noted had been supported by teachers — and his early experiences within his area of the curriculum: he'd 'had to keep those [reflective] skills going very much within myself in this faculty' and seek collaboration outside his department. However, collaboration with a young teacher who had arrived the previous year was changing that; they had 'kind of worked like a team', and, moreover, there had been and were strongly evaluative and questioning colleagues with whom he had collaborated.

> I'm a product of new methodology in many ways, but I don't feel that in any way that has blinkered me to the merits and the great work done by colleagues before some of the recent changes. And very much I look at them and get experience from them, and I think that probably they value me in those kinds of ways as well and I hold that very dear.

V, 1, in an inner-city school, had a colleague who she said was 'brilliant with the kids and the kids love him, because I think he loves them really . . . He . . . says, "Well, I always smile at them in the lesson.

First thing I always do is smile at them. You start the lesson with a smile, you'll be alright". And you know, it's simplistic, but it's actually very true . . .' L, 6 when she was in her second school, an independent, had the task of reviewing the 11–13 history curriculum, ensuring variety of teaching methods as well as content, and,

> produced all the resources that were needed. It was quite exciting because I was in a position to watch my head of department change his teaching methods over the time that I was there and he did become much more flexible in the classroom.

Prior to her leaving the school the two of them 'were doing a lot of team teaching right through the school. We actually shared a first-year class and then we also used to combine our A-level sets as well and do team teaching there.' Here was someone, with whom she got on well, who 'gave [her] a lot of examples'.

First, it was more than simply heartening to know that there are teachers who can rejoice in how their colleagues' attributes are, or can be, of benefit to their own professional development. Such recognition of significance, which may be among beginners' most valuable gifts, is important if a school seeks seriously to develop a collaborative culture. Second, as Hughes (1971, p. 123) points out, 'it takes intelligence to find the others that will bring out the best in one self.' Perhaps we should add breadth of mind and determination. Note that Z, 1 didn't cast himself as a disciple; he had reservations about some matters but he was clear about the merits of his colleague which could, as it were, rub off on him. And S, 2, because people are pushed apart by the ways they are socialized into their different subjects, was having to work hard to distil 'lessons' from his observations.

It is worth being reminded that we can learn, positively, from colleagues whose methods may be deemed to be 'dated'. E, 5 clearly saw his colleagues 'in the round' (see Fullan and Hargreaves, 1992, p. 99) and as a result perceived that he had benefited. Third, I,6 had a signally valuable colleague. In their daily working lives, teachers are continually reinforced as givers of support and advice. Yet for collaboration to be authentic, older and more experienced colleagues 'should acknowledge and communicate their own needs as help-receivers as well as help-givers, . . .' (*ibid.*, p. 57). M, 3 had a colleague who avoided being the 'helping hand that (strikes) again': he assisted without judging. Fourth, who can know who is the best person to work with any particular individual? It is not necessarily someone in the same subject: it is not necessarily someone who is highly visible. Mentoring relationships organized in formal ways must not detract from other, unspecified developments. Perhaps appropriate members of schools' senior management might be wise to make themselves as aware as possible of such developments so that they can be informally and sensitively supported. Finally, do beginners' 'others' know of their significance, of the influence they are having? Brown and McIntyre (1993), who adopted an 'exclusively positive' view when observing lessons, report how the teachers in their study were delighted when the researchers gave them feedback on their pupils' positive opinions of their teaching. This 'came as a pleasant surprise' (p. 31) and they were considerably motivated. It is worth noting for our purposes here that these teachers were surprised even though Brown and McIntyre say they 'undoubtedly worked with a group of people who had particularly good relationships with their pupils' (p. 31). The researchers urge that a refocusing in in-service education on what teachers are doing well would be a greater boost to self-evaluative reflection than a concentration on tackling failings (see pp. 114–15). This seems psychologically appropriate. Perhaps along the same lines, but rather more informally, individuals might ensure that their colleagues know how significant they have been to them and in what ways. This too, could be a pleasant surprise and considerably motivating.

The Place of the Residential

It seems likely that Claxton's statement that 'teaching is in part about putting together clear, interesting, well-judged lessons, but above all it is about relationships' (Claxton, 1990, pp. 16–17) would be widely acceptable. Not surprisingly therefore, and given that 'good standing with pupils is an achievement of immense significance to teachers — especially beginning teachers' (Hull, 1985, p. 6) the highlights perceived by teachers in this study commonly had to do with their relationships with pupils. For some, residential experiences at home and abroad figured strongly here. We have already referred to X, 5's delight in his pupils' reactions to outdoor challenge, and to I, 3's deeply felt experience. Two other accounts may usefully be cited.

N, 1 had a 'very good week' camping with his form pupils. 'It was great. We do everything, we really get stuck in.' Organized activities included canoeing, climbing and archery. In addition, there were plenty of opportunities for pupils 'just being together' . . . 'They made shelters and then they made a camp fire and boiled their own soup and those type of activities where they all muck in' he said. Evening activities included the opportunity to investigate cooperatively whatever had been found of interest, 'or they do some art work or English . . .' This experience had made him look afresh at the quality of his relationships with his pupils . . . He had thought that he and they were close, that they got on. Closer and more sustained contact with them had been revealing. More was learned during the first day, he felt, than would have been the case 'for a couple of years' without this residential experience. There was 'time to listen and tell about family histories, or just things they were interested in'. He was impressed by one significant outcome, 'how many pupils who came out of their shells who have fortunately not gone back in.'

H, 6's experience introduces the tension between 'academic' and 'social worker' in conceptions of teaching. He perceived himself as having been more of an academic entrant to the profession. He recalled that at his first school, in his first year of teaching, and for the first time, he participated in what he described as a 'really good' week's residential with second and third-year pupils. 'In some ways it was really my first . . . sort of very close, intimate experience of working with kids.' He liked the 'joining-in aspect'; he wasn't simply teaching the pupils but 'also doing other things with them'. He enjoyed working in a team with pupils and also working as a member of the staff team. He appreciated the intensiveness of the collaboration between the teachers: it was 'great'. H, 6 actually began his identification of highlights by referring to this residential experience, and although this was justifiable chronologically, it also seems an entirely appropriate prologue to his achievement of what he preferred to call 'a sense of an ultimate kind of satisfaction' rather than a highlight whilst at his second school. 'That was a turning point for me in the sense that I kind of came down off the mountain really, and realized that successfully working with kids of all sorts of abilities does actually mean talking to them and being more open, not sort of being quite so distant, or thinking that you can remain as an authority figure all the time.'

Above all, about relationships? Let's assume with Carr that 'teaching as a job is inextricably implicated in personal relationships'. That is to say, following him, we are talking about more than 'getting on with' pupils, more than 'responsiveness' in the classroom, rather about actuating them beneficially, demonstrating and modelling the worth of a relationship, and 'mak(ing) people better as people by guiding them towards lives which are as decent, rewarding and fulfilling as possible'. (Carr, 1992, pp. 26–27). If this is the case, then Souper's point can hardly be denied, that a secondary school pupil has the right to expect to form a close relationship with at least some of [his teachers]'

(Souper, 1976, p. 55). And if this is so, what sort of opportunities should be provided to enable this to happen? In spite of the funding challenge, arguments for residential experiences for pupils and teachers would appear to be strong (Thomas, 1991; Brighouse, 1991). Appropriately placed in the school year, they may be of particular benefit to beginners and student teachers, and a sound investment in a thoughtful programme of early professional development.

Conclusion

This chapter has taken a celebratory approach to teaching, focusing on highlights of the job as perceived by beginning teachers. Examples have been given. Four aspects have been examined more closely in order to generate questions and observations for those responsible in schools for the successful preparation and induction of entrants to the profession.

Note

1 I would like to thank the twenty-five teachers for participating in this study and the University of Sheffield for financial assistance from its Research Fund.

References

Brighouse, T. (1991) 'One lesson, one week. Is one lesson outdoors worth seven inside? And does one week's residential equal a year of normal schooling?', *Head Teachers Review*, Autumn, pp. 2, 4–5.

Brown, S. and McIntyre, D. (1993) *Making Sense of Teaching*, Buckingham, Open University Press.

Carr, D. (1992) 'Four Dimensions of Educational Professionalism', Westminster Studies in Education, 15, pp. 19–29.

Claxton, G. (1990) *Teaching to Learn: A Direction for Education*, London, Cassell.

Erhard, W. (1984) 'On transformation and productivity: An interview', *ReVISION*, 7, 2, pp. 30–8.

Fullan, M. and Hargreaves, A. (1992) *What's Worth Fighting For In Your School? Working Together for Improvement*, Buckingham, Open University Press in association with the OPSTF.

GRIFFITHS, M. (1993) 'Educational change and the self', *British Journal of Educational Studies*, 41, 2, pp. 150–63.

HOYLE, E. (1986) *The Politics of School Management*, Sevenoaks, Hodder and Stoughton.

HUGHES, E.C. (1971) 'What other?', in ROSE, A.M. (Ed) *Human Behaviour and Social Processes: An Interactionist Approach*, London, Routledge and Kegan Paul, pp. 119–27.

HULL, C. (1985) 'Pupils as teacher educators', *Cambridge Journal of Education*, 15, 1, pp. 1–8.

LITTLE, J.W. (1990) 'The persistence of privacy: Autonomy and initiative in teachers' professional relations', *Teachers College Record*, 91, 4, pp. 509–36.

MASLOW, A.H. (1978) *The Farther Reaches of Human Nature*, Harmondsworth, Penguin.

PASCALE, R. (1990) *Managing on the Edge: How Successful Companies Use Conflict to Stay Ahead*, Harmondsworth, Penguin.

RISEBOROUGH, G.F. and POPPLETON, P. (1991) 'Veterans versus Beginners: A study of teachers at a time of fundamental change in comprehensive schooling', *Educational Review*, 43, 3, pp. 307–34.

RUDDUCK, J. (1993) 'The theatre of daylight: Qualitative research and school profile studies', in SCHRATZ, M. *Qualitative Voices in Educational Research*, London, Falmer Press, pp. 8–22.

SOUPER, P.C. (1976) *About to Teach: An Introduction to Method in Teaching*, London, Routledge and Kegan Paul.

THOMAS, T. (1991) 'Residential centres: An entitlement for all, or an extra curricular experience for the favoured few?', *Head Teachers Review*, Autumn, pp. 8–10.

WILLIAMS, V. (1989) 'Schools and their communities — Issues in external relations', in SAYER, J. and WILLIAMS, V. *Schools and External Relations: Managing the New Partnerships*, London, Cassell, pp. 15–32.

Chapter 3

The Use of Competences in Teacher Education

Geoff Whitty

Introduction

The specification of competences for teaching and other professions is currently receiving official encouragement in the UK and elsewhere but it is also a matter of considerable controversy within the professions concerned[1]. However, competence-based and performance-based approaches to teacher education are by no means new. They were popular in the USA in the 1970s and began to have some impact in the further education (FE) sector in the UK in the early 1980s (Tuxworth, 1982). During the 1980s, they were given fresh impetus by the influence of the National Council for Vocational Qualifications (NCVQ) and by the wider debate about quality in education and training. While these developments were not centrally concerned with teacher education, their potential relevance was recognized by a number of FE teacher-training courses which sought to model themselves on the National Vocational Qualification (NVQ) approach.

Prior to 1990, the use of competence-based approaches in teacher education for the school sector in the UK was rather less developed, although Eraut (1989) had already pointed to their potential and a few BEd and PGCE courses were beginning to show signs of their influence. Meanwhile, critiques of conventional approaches to initial teacher education had led to growing demands that it be both school-based and more directly linked to the competences required of the beginning teacher. The Secretary of State's criteria for initial teacher education contained in Circular 24/89 (DES, 1989) included exit criteria for certain activities within courses of initial teacher education and courses had to meet these in order to be recommended for accreditation by the Council for the Accreditation of Teacher Education (CATE).

The growing official interest in linking qualified teacher status (QTS) to the achievement of certain specified competences initiated a flurry of activity on the part of various agencies and institutions to explore the potential of competence-based approaches to teacher education. The Modes of Teacher Education (MOTE) research project found in 1990–91 that, although only 6 per cent of courses claimed to be based on a competence model of teaching (compared with 72 per cent using a reflective practitioner model), 58 per cent of courses were already making use of competences for various purposes (Barrett *et al.*, 1993).

By 1992, however, the use of competences in designing, undertaking and assessing initial teacher education ceased to be optional in England and Wales. Circular 9/92 (DFE, 1992), which replaced Circular 24/89 for secondary initial training, required higher education institutions, schools and students to 'focus on the competences of teaching throughout the whole period of initial training' and a similar phrase was used in the consultation document and draft circular on primary training issued the following year (DFE, 1993a). These circulars contained 'official' lists of competences organized under the following headings:

Secondary List
- Subject Knowledge
- Subject Application
- Class Management
- Assessment and Recording of Pupils' Progress
- Further Professional Development

Primary List
- Curriculum Content, Planning and Assessment
  - a Whole Curriculum
  - b Subject Knowledge and Application
  - c Assessment and Recording of Pupils' Progress
- Teaching Strategies
  - a Pupils' Learning
  - b Teaching Strategies and Techniques
- Further Professional Development

Although the government now plans to abolish CATE, the agency that currently polices the adherence of institutions to the Secretary of State's criteria, it is inconceivable that the present government and its proposed Teacher Training Agency will abandon the use of competences and it is quite possible that it will extend it (DFE, 1993b).

Nevertheless, teacher-education institutions currently have considerable freedom to decide on the particular approach they take to competences, since the DFE has so far resisted pressure from the Employment Department to bring teacher education into the NCVQ framework. The official list of competences contained in the secondary circular were presented as being no threat to existing ways of using competences being developed in many local areas. Furthermore, the officially-stated view is that the specific competences listed in the circulars 'do not constitute a complete curriculum for teacher education' nor can 'all aspects of a course . . . be described or assessed in [competency] form' (DFE, 1992). There remains, at least in theory and for the time being, some freedom to define and use competences in different ways.

Definitions

In any debate about a value-laden activity such as teacher education, difficulties are bound to be encountered in relation to the key concepts employed. Initially, some British teacher educators rejected the idea of using competences in teacher education on the grounds that it would encourage an over-emphasis on skills and techniques; that it ignored vital components of teacher education; that what informed performance was as important as performance itself; and that the whole was more than the sum of the parts. This rejection was partly a reaction to American checklists of teacher behaviour, such as one scheme in which 121 separate teacher behaviours had to be checked off by an independent observer and fed into a computer to produce a competency level (Gitlin and Smyth, 1989). However, other teacher educators who were equally scathing about such approaches, argued that a 'reflective practitioner' model of teaching, which often claims to be the very antithesis of a technicist and behaviourist view of teaching, could itself be expressed in competence terms. Hextall *et al.* (1991, p. 15), for example, argued that 'teaching is not reducible to a set of technical operations' but then went on to say that they were not 'running away from the issue of the systematic appraisal of teaching competence' and that even the quality of reflectivity could be formulated as a series of competences that could be monitored.

When the Council for National Academic Awards looked at the early use of competences in teacher education course submissions (CNAA, 1992; Whitty and Willmott, 1991), it found that there was considerable confusion about the use of the term. Where course teams were at all explicit about what the term 'competence' was meant to convey, two major approaches to its definition could be discerned:

- competence characterized as an ability to perform a task satisfactorily, the task being clearly defined and the criteria of success being set out alongside this;

- competence characterized as wider than this, encompassing intellectual, cognitive and attitudinal dimensions, as well as performance; in this model, neither competences nor the criteria of achievement are so readily susceptible to sharp and discrete identification.

Thus, one school of thought, behaviourist if you like, defines competences in terms of a series of behaviours or performances of which the execution at an acceptable level can readily be identified by observation. In this model individual competences are identified by analysis of tasks and roles, and the analysis proceeds by breaking down competent performance into a number of discrete parts. Even when an attempt is made to include underpinning knowledge and understanding, these tend to be presented in terms of additional discrete competences.

The superficial attractions of this approach are considerable. It simplifies what may have been a complicated series of actions, and for purposes of training it makes them amenable to specific practice and discussion. However, it takes little account of the fact that in real life a competence can be applied only within specific contexts. These will vary considerably according to circumstances, and in order to perform successfully a practitioner needs to be able to respond to new situations in a way which goes beyond a decontextualized set of practised procedures. The approach is also open to the criticism that such a varied and diffuse activity as teaching cannot properly be seen as nothing more than the sum of a number of discrete behaviours. When we observe an outstanding teacher at work, the whole often does seem to be more than the sum of the parts.

So the other approach is to assign much greater importance to the part played by knowledge, understanding and attitudes as central to the whole process of developing professional competence, and to view them as permeating and affecting practice in an integrative and holistic way. In higher-level activities, knowledge and understanding are involved even in very specific and particular performances. One advantage of applying this perspective to teaching is that it can accommodate the strong dimension of values which is present in professional activities of this nature. It can thereby provide the basis for elaborating a fully developed concept of the reflective practitioner (McElvogue and Salters, 1992).

However, adopting this approach has its own disadvantages. The list of necessary competences either increases or has to be expressed at a very high level of generality. Assessment becomes considerably more complex and needs to go beyond the assessment of observable workplace skills. Nevertheless, unlike simplistic checklists of teacher behaviour, this approach avoids placing inappropriate constraints on the professional judgment of teachers and teacher educators.

It is usually argued that NVQs entail the first approach, while a high-level professional occupation like teaching can only operate with the broader approach to competences. In trying to extend its NVQs to higher-level professional occupations, NCVQ are currently grappling with the tensions between the two models and it is not yet clear whether they can be made compatible. According to the NCVQ (1989, p. 4):

- the area of competence to be covered must have meaning and relevance in the context of the occupational structure in the sector of employment concerned;
- the statement of competence must be based on an analysis of occupational roles within the area of competence to which it relates;
- the statement of competence must encompass the underpinning knowledge and understanding required for effective performance in employment.

While this last statement extends the notion of competence beyond observable workplace skills, it does not necessarily encompass all the elements of personal and professional education which may be the concern of courses of teacher education. Whether the broader aims of teacher education can be accommodated within a competence-based approach may well depend on how broad a definition of competence is employed. A narrow definition based on observable workplace skills is certainly in some tension with the rationale of a liberal education and even with the notion of the reflective professional.

In teacher education in the UK, though, there has not yet been much pressure to force everything into an NVQ straitjacket. Many teacher educators are therefore taking the position that, if they can find ways of working with competences that meet the government's criteria without sacrificing a commitment to deeper professional values, they may yet avoid the worst excesses of the original NVQ approach. More positively, some argue that, properly used, competences can actually help to enhance the quality of the professional education of teachers and help to remove some of the mystique that has too often surrounded teacher education in the past.

The dilemma facing teacher educators is not confined to the UK. A similar debate about the possibilities and problems of using competences in teacher education is currently taking place in Australia. On the one hand, John Smyth of Flinders University argues against going down a road that seems to be derived from a behaviourist model of learning and which is intended to control teachers and demean their professional status (Smyth, 1993). On the other hand, Jim Walker and Barbara Preston (Walker, 1991; Preston and Walker, 1993) have suggested that it is better to embrace an acceptable version of competences than to reject them entirely. They argue that professional activities can be expressed as competences, providing competences are sufficiently broadly defined. Yet, in some ways, these two commentaries are not as far apart as it seems. Smyth rejects the approach of the Standards Framework of the National Training Board, Australia's equivalent of Britain's NCVQ while, in proposing an alternative holistic approach to competences, Walker and Preston too reject the essentially behaviourist approach of that body.

The Northern Ireland Exercise

Thus, in both the UK and Australia, teacher educators are exploring ways of using competences to assist the professional development of teachers without undermining traditional professional values. I was recently involved in such an exercise in Northern Ireland, where I chaired a working party on competences which included representatives from the higher education institutions, education and library boards and teachers. Our terms of reference required us to define the competences which characterize the successful professional teacher and to consider their relative importance, their use and their assessment. We were also asked to consider how their development should be phased across initial teacher training, induction and further professional development, and suggest the balance between higher education institutions and schools in their development.

While conscious of the unresolved debates about the definition of competences and their application referred to above, the working group was also aware that most people in teacher education did now recognize that there could be some benefits in using competences in certain aspects of teacher education. In the Northern Ireland context, where (as in England and Wales) teacher educators were required to work within the CATE framework, we took the view that, if our proposals were to be workable, they would need to bear a recognizable relationship to the 'official' categories of competence listed in the government circulars.

However, we also felt that neither these broad categories nor the individual competences listed within them were adequate for our purposes. Although they were not intended to define the whole curriculum of initial teacher training, we considered that some omissions needed remedying. Indeed, on balance, the working group felt that the disadvantages of producing a longer list of competences were outweighed by the dangers of anything not on the list being relegated to second-class status and regarded as dispensable when resources were under pressure. With my colleagues on the Modes of Teacher Education project, I had already encountered widespread concern in England and Wales that not only traditional educational studies work, but also reflective practice, would be expunged from initial teacher education as a result of the limitation of the official lists. There was particular unease about the implication that such things as special educational needs and even critical awareness were hitherto to be concerns for further professional development rather than pre-service training.

Although we started with the CATE list of competences, the working group looked to other sources in order to elaborate — as our terms of reference required — a specification of the competences required of the successful professional teacher. Given its provenance in initial teacher training, the list of competences in Circular 9/92 was not particularly helpful in defining those to be developed during induction and further professional development. Neither time nor other resources were available for us to undertake the sort of task analysis, functional analysis or other research activities that have been used to develop competence-based education and training in other fields. We had to rely instead on secondary sources supplemented by the ideas and experience of the working group itself and of those whom it had an opportunity to consult.

Our terms of reference had drawn our attention to the work of the Scottish Office Education Department (SOED), and we found their notes of guidance helpful in refining and augmenting the list of competences to be developed within the phase of initial training. Like the SOED (1992), we took the view that the term 'professional competences' should be taken to refer to knowledge, understanding and attitudes as well as to practical skills. We agreed with their view that in order to teach satisfactorily certain craft skills have undoubtedly to be learnt. We agreed too that teachers must in addition to this have a knowledge and understanding both of the content of their teaching and of the processes which they are carrying out, and be able to evaluate and justify their actions. We added that they also need an appreciation of the broader context in which they are working.

We decided that a simple list of competences, no matter how comprehensive and well structured, could not convey the totality of what we wanted to say about the professional competence of a teacher.

One of the criticisms often made of competence-based approaches to education and training, and to professional education and training in particular, is that the atomization of professional knowledge, judgment and skill into discrete competences inevitably fails to capture the essence of professional competence. One way to meet the objection would be to specify some generic professional competences. This approach has been adopted in respect of police training by John Elliott and his colleagues working at the University of East Anglia (Elliott, 1992). For similar reasons, a project concerned with social work training run by Richard Winter at Anglia Polytechnic University has chosen to specify a number of core assessment criteria which bind together the individual competences which it has identified (Winter and Maisch, 1991). The principles underlying such work were highly influential in our thinking, even though our detailed proposals diverged from it in significant ways. They are also similar to those being advocated by Jim Walker in Australia.

One way to deal with the problem might have been to incorporate at the end of the list of specific knowledge and skills, a section entitled 'professional attitudes' or 'competences related to professionalism'. This is essentially how the Scottish scheme deals with the problem. But the items under this heading are really of a different order from those under the other headings. In some ways, they are more in the nature of personal qualities or the general (and perhaps ideal) characteristics of successful teachers which permeate all their specific competences and enable them to apply these appropriately.

The Identification of Competences

We therefore ended up with two sets of qualities which we look for in a successful professional teacher — what we termed 'professional characteristics' and 'professional competences'. Professional characteristics were what we considered to be the underlying qualities of the teacher which enable him or her to pull the individual competences together and apply them in the professional context. In describing the characteristics in this way we were not, of course, suggesting that they are innate, and that 'good teachers are born and not made': these qualities too can be fostered and developed. Our suggested list related to the following aspects of professional activity:

Professional characteristics of the successful teacher:

1 Professional values;
2 Professional development;

3 Personal development;
4 Communication and relationships; and
5 Synthesis and application.

This list had then to be read along with our list of specific competences, which we divided into professional knowledge and understanding and professional skills, as follows:

Professional competences of the successful teacher:

1. Knowledge and understanding
1.1 Knowledge of children and their learning;
1.2 Subject knowledge;
1.3 Knowledge of the curriculum;
1.4 Knowledge of the education system; and
1.5 Knowledge of the teacher's role.
2. Skills
2.1 Subject application;
2.2 Classroom methodology;
2.3 Class management;
2.4 Assessment and recording; and
2.5 Undertaking the wider role.

We envisaged the two statements as interlocking with each other. This could either be seen as a matrix with professional characteristics permeating the performance of professional competences — or it might be represented graphically as in the diagram in Appendix 1. Either way, we were trying to indicate that the professional characteristics of the teacher ought to permeate the application of the specific competences identified under the headings of professional knowledge and professional skills. We wanted to insist to our political masters that a professional teacher requires both.

Phasing and Location

We also made some preliminary suggestions about which of the competences should receive particular attention during the successive phases of ITT, induction and the early years of in-service education. Some competence schemes have discrete lists of competences for ITT and INSET. But, given that the Northern Ireland group took a developmental view of competences rather than one expressed in terms of minimum thresholds, we did not see any of the competences as entirely disposed of at the end of ITT. Instead, we tried to indicate priorities for development at the respective stages rather than to imply that a competence should be entirely neglected in any of them. The competences were assigned letter codes to indicate the stages at which most attention should be given to their development. Letter 'A' indicates initial training, letter 'B' induction and letter 'C' the early years of further professional development. A capital letter is used to signify that a particular phase of training should have a principal responsibility for the competence in question, while a lower case letter suggests that the phase should have a significant but subsidiary role in its development. The page from our report, attached in Appendix 1, gives a flavour of our approach, though the specific codings suggested are, of course, open to debate. It should be noted that, since our remit referred to 'the early stages of in-service training', we did not make any recommendations about the development of school-management competences, such as those specified in the work of the School Management Competences Project in England (Earley, 1992), nor did we refer to the role of teachers in the training of other teachers.

The Northern Ireland group also made suggestions about where the individual competences might best be developed, though these related to the particular conditions of Northern Ireland and do not reflect the extent of the move towards school-based training that is now taking place in England. They are anyway preliminary thoughts on the subject. As can be seen in the examples in Appendix 1, we employed a five-point scale to indicate the amount of school experience that we believe is required to develop the respective competences. Those which are scored '1' require little or no school experience, while those scored '5' could be developed wholly in a school, with no explicit input from outside. Others require both a structured input (tutoring, guidance or support) and a greater or lesser degree of classroom experience or practice. Thus '2' may be taken to mean that a competence can be developed largely outside the classroom, but requires trainee teachers to have experience on which to draw in order to develop full understanding. '3' means that development requires roughly equal amounts of work inside and outside the classroom, and '4' that it requires substantial experience and practice in the classroom supplemented by appropriate guidance and support.

This sort of analysis, though often contentious in detail, can help clarify a division of labour in partnerships between higher education and schools. In practice, though, the Northern Ireland group took the view that the development of very few of the competences could be the *exclusive* preserve of either higher education institutions or schools.

Course Design

The Northern Ireland working group did not engage in course design. That was a responsibility left to another group and to individual institutions and their partner schools. The specification of competences does not of itself imply that courses should take a particular form. Indeed, the philosophy underlying extreme versions of competence-based education suggests that, providing a student can demonstrate a competence, he or she can gain credit for it without having followed a course at all. Such a strategy places the entire burden of assuring the attainment of the required standards on the assessment process. It has also been suggested that students might be permitted to leave a course of initial teacher education and enter teaching once they have reached a certain threshold of competence (Hargreaves, 1989). There are, though, legitimate concerns about the extent to which this approach can undermine the experience of a coherent programme of study, often seen as a necessary part of teacher eduction. However these issues are resolved, courses designed to help students develop particular competences will clearly need to make use of these competences as a vital tool in curricular planning. Competences can usefully be grouped into modules for the purposes of curricular design and assessment, as has been done in the Anglia social-work project to which reference was made earlier (Winter and Maisch, 1991).

The extent to which exit competences will inform course design in teacher education will vary. Prior to the requirements of Circular 9/92, most course teams used the approach only for parts of their courses and it is perhaps not surprising that the most extensive use of competences has been in relation to school experience. Indeed, some tutors believe that, in principle, the approach should be limited to this area, particularly where a narrow definition of competences is being used. Other course teams, usually working with a broader definition, have tried to adopt a competence-based approach to a whole course. School-based courses, of course, provide an obvious opportunity for trying to relate all elements of a course to the achievement of workplace competences.

At present, the specific competences used in course design can be derived from a variety of sources. In addition to the competences specified in government circulars, the various task analyses of teaching or attempts to specify the attributes of the teacher as professional might be one starting point. In other cases, they might be determined by the staff designing the courses, probably in consultation with teachers and LEA advisors. There is also considerable scope for students to negotiate the competences which they wish the course to help them develop and this is likely to be a central feature of INSET provision which is based on the use of competences.

Teaching, Learning and Assessment

Despite claims that competence-based approaches emphasize outcomes at the expense of processes, Jessup (1991, p. 138) argues that the whole point of specifying outcomes is to promote learning. If competence-based approaches encourage teacher educators to be more explicit about the characteristics of skilled professionalism that they seek to encourage, this is likely to have implications for teaching and learning. In some cases, it will lead to whole-course policies on teaching and learning. In theory, courses designed with an emphasis on exit competences might be expected to be non-prescriptive about the methods used to encourage their attainment. Indeed, they should provide considerable scope for the negotiation of teaching and learning methods. In practice, teaching methods are likely to be influenced by the particular definition of competences adopted and by the actual competences being encouraged. The competences required of the reflective teacher are likely to require rather different methods of teaching and learning from those of the instructor.

The early association of competence-based approaches with vocational training, especially in some of the narrowly behavioural approaches adopted in the USA, has sometimes led to a view amongst teacher educators that competence-based education implies an instructional form of pedagogy. A narrowly skills-based definition of competence has, as in earlier courses based upon behavioural objectives, sometimes led to teaching that stresses performance at the expense of understanding. The early work of NCVQ was criticized for similar excesses, but it is now accepted that such an approach is inappropriate to the development of higher-level professional skills.

This has obvious implications for assessment. NCVQ now acknowledges that for levels four and above, it may be necessary to assess underpinning knowledge and understanding separately from workplace performance. One of the last acts of the Training Agency was to mount a research project on the assessment of underpinning knowledge and understanding because it was recognized that, while knowledge was essential to performance, it could not always be inferred from direct observation in the workplace. Interestingly, the report of that study has never been published.

It is certainly likely that in a field such as teacher education a range of assessment methods will need to be employed, even in courses based around the achievement of workplace competences. Definitions of competence that go beyond skills to include knowledge, values and attitudes raise particular problems for assessment. There is controversy over whether competence-based assessment raises any more problems of validity and reliability than more conventional academic approaches, but the arguments are by no means decisive (Jessup, 1991; Gonczi, 1994). Whatever approaches are adopted, we need to acknowledge that the attainment of competences requires inferences to be made on the basis of a range of evidence; the less specific the criteria enunciated, the higher the level of inference will be and the more informed the judgment that will be called for. One strategy for attempting to ensure that the competences being assessed are not based on too narrow an experiential context is to specify range indicators which describe the context within which a performance should take place; for example, a student-teacher may be required to demonstrate practical ability in more than one type of school.

The competences specified in some courses are the minimum or threshold competences necessary to perform particular teaching activities and, in others, those characteristic of the 'good teacher'. There are also differing views about whether a competence is something that is either a specific achievement or, alternatively, a dimension of performance in terms of which one can perform at different levels. In the former case, one might expect distinct lists of competences for ITT and INSET courses, while the latter approach implies a similar (or overlapping) list of competences with different levels of attainment. This was the approach adopted in Northern Ireland. Specialist courses may, of course, use a restricted range of competences or introduce additional ones. Courses in education management, for example, draw upon generic management competences.

A major issue for teacher education which leads to higher education awards and to qualified-teacher status is how to decide how the assessment of individual competences relates to the criteria used in making the overall award. In hybrid courses the relationship of the assessment of competences to any other forms of assessment employed on a course also needs to be clarified. Here again, the social-work courses developed at Anglia Polytechnic University provide a possible model (Winter and Maisch, 1991).

Profiling

Even though the Northern Ireland schedule of competences embodied a substantial number of individual items, some of which are clearly more specific than others, the list remains at a fairly high level of generality. We took the view that it was neither feasible nor desirable to sub-divide these competences into even narrower technical and behavioural components, even though our terms of reference required it. Although they are mainly expressed in behavioural terms, few if any of them amount to precise measurable statements of performance criteria. This is because professional competences tend not to be susceptible to discrete measurement and the form in which these might be assessed will depend to some extent on the locus of training.

Nevertheless, the specification of competences lends itself to relatively clear reporting of assessments for both students and potential employers. It is therefore highly compatible with current trends towards the use of profiles in teacher-education courses. Like other approaches to profiling, the use of competences can be formative and/or summative and it raises similar concerns about ownership of the profile of achievement, an issue that could become particularly significant in the context of teacher appraisal.

The official view in Scotland appears to be that it is for institutions and their partner schools to decide how each competence should be assessed (SOED, 1992). The SOED also suggests that there may be a case for nationally defined performance criteria, but the lack of professional consensus about what these criteria might be makes such a task difficult to undertake at the present time. The Northern Ireland group was of the opinion that it would be better for any such generally agreed criteria to emerge out of work done at local level by partnerships between higher education institutions and schools as they attempt to operationalize and assess the competences. Similarly, we felt that student self-assessment schedules and profile statements might best be developed through a sharing of good practice amongst the various partners in the training process.

In England, though, it now seems that we are to have a common national framework for such profiles (DFE, 1993b). But, whatever form this eventually takes, it is to be hoped that the profile statements will refer to what the Northern Ireland group defined as professional characteristics as well as to professional competences.

Conclusion

My experience of the exercise in Northern Ireland was that it was seen as an extremely fruitful one by the various parties involved, including some who were initially suspicious or sceptical about the use of competences in teacher education. It provided an important opportunity for partners to think through issues together and to develop a common framework for thinking about their roles. Most members of the group felt that the process of thinking through the issues had helped to demystify teacher education, provide clearer goals for students, point to a clearer definition of the roles of schools and institutions and provide a firmer base for induction and further professional development. And, despite widespread unease among teacher educators about narrow behaviourist approaches to the specification and assessment of competences, the approach adopted, by recognizing the importance of generic professional competences as well as specific classroom skills, appears to have commanded widespread support in Northern Ireland. How much of it will be implemented is now a matter for government decision.

Nevertheless, I am still of the view that the advantages of using a full-blown competence-based approach to teacher education remain to be proven, and that it seems unlikely to be the panacea that its staunchest advocates often imply. Most institutional schemes are still at an early stage of development, except perhaps in the field of FE teacher training. I believe there is still insufficient experience to date to justify the national imposition of a uniform approach, but there is considerable scope for further local and regional exploration and evaluation of the range of approaches that has so far developed.

Note

1 This chapter has been compiled from papers developed with other members of a working party of the Council for National Academic Awards (CNAA) on 'Competence-based Approaches to Teacher Education' and a working group on 'Competences' established by the Department of Education in Northern Ireland (DENI) in connection with a review of initial teacher training in the province. Other members of the CNAA working party were

M. Cornish, S. Goulding, W. Harlen, S. Jardine, A.E. Mason, D.W. Pyle, K.B. Wilson, J. Turner, D. Sutherland, L. Wharfe and E.G. Willmott. Other members of the DENI working group were G. Colohan, C. Coxhead, S.I. Davidson, A.E.A. Lamb, D.G. MacIntyre, A. Magee, P. Maguire, S. Marriott, M.G. Salters, R. Small, T. Stewart, M. Matchett and I. Hamilton.

References

Barrett, L., Barton, L., Furlong, J., Galvin, C., Miles, S. and Whitty, G. (1993) *Initial Teacher Education in England and Wales: A Topography*, London, University of London, Goldsmiths College.

CNAA (1992) *Competence-based approaches to teacher education: viewpoints and issues*, London, CNAA.

DFE (1992) *Initial Teacher Training (Secondary Phase) (Circular 9/92)*, London, HMSO.

DFE (1993a) *The Government's Proposals for the Reform of Initial Teacher Training*, London, HMSO.

DFE (1993b) *The Initial Training of Primary School Teachers: New Criteria for Course Approval (Draft Circular)*, London, HMSO.

DES (1989) *Initial Teacher Training: Approval of Courses (Circular 24/89)*, London, HMSO.

Earley, P. (1992) *The School Management Competences Project: Final Report*, Slough, School Management South.

Elliott, J. (1992) 'The Role of a Small Scale Research Project in Developing a Competency-based Police Training Curriculum', Norwich, University of East Anglia.

Eraut, M. (1989) 'Initial teacher training and the NVQ model', in: Burke, J.W. (Ed) *Competency based Education and Training*, Lewes, Falmer Press.

Gitlin, A. and Smyth, J. (1989) *Teacher Evaluation: Educative Alternatives*, Lewes, Falmer Press.

Gonczi, A. (1994) 'Competency based assessment in the professions in Australia', *Assessment in Education*, 1, 1, pp. 27–45.

Hargreaves, D. (1989) 'PGCE assessment fails the test', *The Times Educational Supplement*, 3 November.

Hextall, I., Lawn, M., Menter, I., Sidgwick, S. and Walker, S. (1991) *Imaginative Projects: Arguments for a New Teacher Education*, London, Goldsmiths' College.

Jessup, G. (1991) *Outcomes: NVQs and the Emerging Model of Education and Training*, Lewes, Falmer Press.

McElvogue, M. and Salters, M. (1992) 'Models of Competence and Teacher Training', Belfast, the Queen's University of Belfast.

NCVQ (1989) *National Vocational Qualifications: Criteria and Procedures*, London, National Council for Vocational Qualifications.

Preston, B. and Walker, J. (1993) 'Competency based standards in the professions and higher education: a holistic approach,' Mimeo, University of Canberra.

SMYTH, J. (1993) 'The competence approach to teaching: do we need it in its current form?', *South Australian Educational Leader*, 4, 4, pp. 1–6.

SOED (1992) *Initial Teacher Training: Draft Revised Guidelines for Teacher Training Courses*, Edinburgh, Scottish Office Education Department.

TUXWORTH, E.N. (1982) *Competency in Teaching: A Review of Competency and Performance-based Staff Development*, London, Further Education Curriculum Review and Development Unit.

WALKER, J. (1991) 'A general rationale and conceptual approach to the application of competency based standards in teaching', Paper presented to the conference of the Australian Teacher Education Association.

WHITTY, G. and WILLMOTT, E. (1991) 'Competence-based teacher education: Approaches and issues', *Cambridge Journal of Education*, 21, 3, pp. 309–18.

WINTER, R. and MAISCH, M. (1991) *The ASSET Programme*, 1 and 2, Chelmsford, Anglia Polytechnic/Essex Social Services Department.

Chapter 4

Partnership: The Leicester Secondary Experience

Richard Aplin

Working Relationships with Schools

There has been at Leicester a long and successful tradition of schools and university working together in partnership on issues concerned with initial teacher education. Its roots can be traced to the appointment of designated teacher-tutors in schools in the time of Brian Simon, but it also includes the work undertaken in IT-INSET by Pat Ashton and colleagues in the Centre for Evaluation and Development in Teacher Education, based in Leicester. Both these strands, each developed over a substantial period, and running alongside each other, have had a direct and identifiable influence on the development of the present Secondary Partnership Scheme, which has been in existence since its initial pilot in 1989.

One of the features common to the three schemes is the recognition that a student teacher is one of a number of participants in a complex interweaving of processes from which all should be able to benefit in distinctive ways. Thus, although the principal focus is appropriately on the student teacher whose professional development is at the centre of the operation, there are benefits to be gained by the experienced colleagues involved in that operation, whether they have their principal activity in a secondary school or in an institution of higher education.

Brian Simon was able to describe as early as 1966 'a fruitful relationship between the university and practising teachers in different schools', in which 'those acting as teacher-tutors in a particular subject — say, history, biology or physics — may meet regularly for discussions at the School of Education, discussions which have extended to cover new developments in teaching the subject, research under way, as well as the tutorial function itself'. (Simon, 1980)

The notion of a team of professionals was to the forefront in the IT-INSET work which exploited the various motives of the different participants, and was held to be a response to the guidance offered by CATE in helping institutions meet the requirements of DES Circular 3/84.

> The most effective partnership arrangements between institutions and schools are often those which have been designed with the needs of students, trainers and teachers equally in mind. (CATE, 1986)

> The IT-INSET model, which is actually cited in *Catenote* No 4, does indeed address the needs of students, trainers and teachers equally. (Everton and Impey, 1989)

This is not to say that there is not common experience built into the model. The tasks carried out by the team members were shared. A team was composed of a teacher from the school, a group of PGCE student teachers, usually about six, and a university tutor. Recognizing the primacy of the class teacher's role in working with the class, it was up to the class teacher to identify the focus of concern, but once that particular decision had been made, all members of the team participate in all aspects of the team's work:

- they plan the work as a team;
- they share the teaching and observations in the classroom;
- they evaluate the relevance and value of what pupils have gained from each session;
- they reflect on what has been learned;
- they use this in planning the next stage. (Everton and Impey, 1989)

The experience could be stimulating for all participants. Adrian Stokes's account gives a flavour of the level of discussion, from a student teacher perspective:

> Despite, or perhaps because of, the difficulties we encountered in operating as a team within the classroom, our collaboration outside the classroom was intense and stimulating. In tackling the questions that arose in the lessons, a high level of co-operation and commitment was achieved. Although some, of course, talked more than others, all made regular contributions

to the discussion and interest was maintained throughout the ten-week programme. (Everton and Impey, 1989)

Pilot and Progress from 1989 to 1991

The influences of the teacher-tutor scheme and IT-INSET are worth highlighting, because the kind of cooperative relationships which they engendered, and which could to a certain extent be taken for granted in local schools, were of major significance in the establishment of a partnership pilot scheme in 1989.

In September of that year, approximately one-third of the PGCE secondary intake at Leicester, composed of student teachers in English and communications, mathematics, modern languages, science and social science, adopted a course pattern at variance with that followed by the remainder, whose course followed the traditional pattern. The new group, led by five subject tutors, fulfilled the existing PGCE course requirements, but in a pattern which was provided alongside the normal operation. So, there were parallel administrative arrangements for the discrete partnership group, who for most of the year were attached to a group of designated partnership schools. This group of schools, for the sake of coherence and simplicity, would not at the same time accept PGCE student teachers from the other cohort.

The partnership arrangements covered two terms of the year. The five tutors continued to provide their normal main subject courses at the university, which took up one day. The other day traditionally devoted to subject work was held in the partnership school, where student teachers were placed in a subject department in pairs. But this two-day allocation of subject work, one in the university and one in school, applied to both cohorts of student teachers at least in the Spring term in 1989–90. Those student teachers who were not in partnership schools participated in IT-INSET work in groups during the school-based subject day, the choice of school being a matter for subject tutor to negotiate with schools.

The major structural difference for the partnership group was that their placement in the school was not only within their subject area, in pairs, but in a cross-curricular group, with the university tutor and school's professional tutor (traditionally an important feature of Leicestershire secondary schools) playing a part in treatment of issues beyond the confines of the subject. Each of the five participating tutors acted as a link tutor with a geographical cluster of schools which were experienced in co-operating and working together. This clustering arrangement had a particular significance in the county, as it took account of the unusual age break in much of Leicestershire's secondary provision. (The LEA is dominated in its provision by a pattern of 11–14 and 14–18 schools.) Clustering not only provided a means of ensuring contact with the whole of the secondary age range, but on a more practical level also helped the link tutor to coordinate the work of student teachers in a group of schools within reasonable constraints.

The first extended block teaching practice for student teachers, late in the Autumn term, was in the partnership school. Even within this restricted partnership model, there were further pragmatic complications. In science, as the partnership student teachers comprised only a third of the science group, the subject course had to be common with the non-partnership cohort.

The English and communications course had an important FE element, necessitating a placement in an FE establishment. As FE colleges were unable to accept student-teacher placements in the Summer term, English and communications student teachers were able only to participate partly in the partnership arrangements, as their Autumn block practice had to be in an FE college. These complications were compounded in 1990–1, when English and communications had to withdraw temporarily from partnership as the course was required to recruit a larger intake, which could not then be accommodated within that year's partnership schools.

It will be understood how essential the experience of local cooperation and understanding between partners was, in order to cope with the variable constraints on the early pilot. Remarkably, however, the arrangements were considered to be sound enough to double the extent of partnership in 1990–1, (tutors, schools and student teachers) when the traditional model became that of the minority of the PGCE cohort, and then to move totally to a partnership version for 1991–2. In order to provide fully for the non-partnership group in 1990–1, a special programme had to be devised for their cross-curricular work, which now involved a smaller number of tutors, for the balance of provision had now altered. Rather than the partnership cohort having to comply with the traditional requirements, it was now seen as the reverse. As may be expected, during the course, whatever group a student teacher was not part of was deemed to have preferential treatment! However, the external examiners found at the end of the year a much more enthusiastic endorsement of their experience by student teachers in the partnership group.

Much of the underlying model implied by parts of DFE Circular

9/92 (DFE, 1992) had therefore already been in place for up to three years at Leicester by the time the document appeared.

Issues Arising from the Development before the Appearance of Circular 9/92

An evaluation of the first-year pilot was conducted by Mike Price, a tutor who was not directly connected then with the partnership arrangements. Considering the concurrent timescale of pilot, evaluation and development of the scheme into a larger cohort with a view to increasing to the whole intake, time was not available to make immediate adaptations to every development in line with the evaluation findings. With the benefit of hindsight, we might think that we were thus unwittingly preparing for a style of innovation and reform to which the British education world has unfortunately become accustomed. Nevertheless, the overall direction in which the partnership scheme developed followed broadly the findings of the Price report.

The evaluation report highlighted areas which it was thought required careful consideration by the School of Education, existing and potential partnership schools, and the Leicestershire LEA, which at that time was in a position to have a considerable influence on the development, not least in providing a limited level of funding to participating schools.

One was 'the articulation of the aims and objectives of partnership and [. .] the working out of purposeful and coherent programmes in individual school circumstances' (Price, 1990). It was recognized that it would be possible to produce 'programmes which are overcomplex to manage, overburdening for teachers and students, and lacking in a clear sense of purpose and coherence overall' (Price, 1990).

In one sense, it was accepted that a more explicit level of documentation would be necessary than had originally been envisaged, as the number of participants became greater, and the possibilities for variation became correspondingly more frequent. By involving more schools, and therefore more personnel from within them in the training of the student teachers, it was necessary to provide at least a minimal written description of roles and responsibilities so that the individual contributions given to the scheme could at least be moving in parallel. (Since the need to implement Circular 9/92, this has taken on a different aspect, as the notion of contractual responsibilities has arisen.) Such a development was seen as a high priority, and the quality of subsequent documentation produced by the university for the course participants and personnel has been seen by a number of external observers as one of the key factors in the scheme's later success. As well as descriptions of the mechanics of the course structures and procedures, and in an attempt to retain the notion of benefits for all, a taxonomy of benefits for all participants (student teacher, school tutor and university tutor) has been presented in each subsequent version of the annual course handbook. The LEA's interest, mentioned above, arose primarily from an awareness of the potential benefits for teachers' own professional development in operating as part of the partnership scheme. Tutors in the university were able to consider the potential of partnership in responding to the requirement to maintain 'recent and relevant' experience in school classrooms.

Specific documents setting out suggested ways in which co-tutors and professional tutors in schools might exercise their roles have also been provided, updated each year to fit the changing circumstances of that particular year's pattern.

Another aspect of the pilot identified in the report was the

> clear need to establish a system of organization and communication which is workable, well-defined, and understood by all the participants. This applies particularly to the School of Education and its relationships with schools generally, but it also applies to individual schools and schools within a cluster. (Price, 1990)

One must recall that during the pilot year, two different modes of PGCE secondary work were in existence. The traditional model, with its communication systems firmly located within harmonious relationships between subject tutors and individual teachers in certain school departments relied upon a way of working which responded to a relatively informal set of expectations. Partnership was more formally structured, based on family groupings of schools, and with an underlying imperative of consistency made necessary by the attachment of link tutors who maintained communications with a group of schools for students both inside and outside their own subject groups. The implications for university tutors for changing their practice, and particularly in surrendering subject autonomy were in some cases quite problematic. At a more mundane level, the potential confusion as to who contacted whom for which reason was actually more widespread than intended. Fortunately, good relationships between tutors and between schools and the university helped to minimize the deleterious effect of some of the misunderstandings, but the emphasis on developing a coherent and consistent system was a major focus for development from 1990 onwards. It was agreed that the axis between link tutor and professional tutor would be the norm for communication, and generally this was successful. Nevertheless, it has to be recognized that a certain *ad hoc* nature typified some of the exchanges between personnel, with resultant potential for further confusion. There was general recognition that the model was evolutionary.

A major issue was that of resource implications. Price reported that

> it is essential that sufficient time is made available for professional tutors, co-tutors and other teachers to set up arrangements for partnership; for planning and supporting the work with students; and for evaluating the outcomes, both formatively and summatively. Arrangements will need to be worked out with the LEA to provide adequate supply cover, with a level of investment which fairly reflects the potential benefits of partnership to the schools concerned. (Price, 1990)

It is significant that this issue of time resources and the use to which such time might be put continued to be a major issue well into 1993, and had a particular place in the post-9/92 negotiations in the formulation of contracts. The greater the level of analysis of roles and responsibilities, the clearer the need for specified time to be made available. The greater the transfer of responsibility for training to the schools, the greater the uncertainty about schools' ability and willingness to devote the necessary time to the role, and to maintain the level of quality of provision that the pre-9/92 partnership scheme was founded upon.

In relation to planning for the future, Price identified the need for the establishment of a steering group, which should include appropriate representation of the interests of the LEA, professional tutors, and the School of Education. He concluded that 'without the support of the LEA, the potential for the development of the concept of partnership will be seriously limited' (Price, 1990).

This was a relatively unproblematic recommendation to implement, and an invited group constituted along the lines of the suggested composition set to work in 1990 in an informal steering role, meeting on an occasional basis. This proved a valuable forum for discussing potential directions for the course arrangements to take, and was invaluable in giving a semi-formalized link with a high level of LEA involvement, which was indeed crucial in enabling a limited amount of resource support to participating schools before the onset of the funds made available through the UFC/HEFCE transitional funding.

This semi-formalized status was both advantageous and a problem. With only a marginal status in relation to university and LEA structures, it could officially be no more than a forum for consultation, without real power to carry through its recommendations. As an informal vehicle, it could be as flexible as necessary in the circumstances, and permitted a more open exchange of views than perhaps a formal committee could have allowed, which, at this early stage in developments led to a fuller mutual understanding of the positions of all parties.

The Partnership Steering Group had the issue of resources as a high priority, and also concerned itself with issues of consistency. The timing of the partnership developments, concurrent with the first stages of the government's dismantling of the traditional role of LEAs, with all the uncertainties which that created both for their personnel and within schools, highlighted the resources question starkly. It became clear that with so many increasing calls on a diminishing local discretion to support ventures, and despite its moral support, hopes that the LEA would be able to increase its financial support for the scheme were unrealistic. At the same time, members of the group were keen to establish a form of consistency within the schools so that a common pattern of provision could be guaranteed, partly to ensure that the student teachers could be certain of their entitlement, but also so that the teachers in schools would all be moving securely in the same direction.

At this stage, a descriptive statement of the role of the co-tutor was produced, taking note of the varying forms of good practice which had been noted in schools, and partly acting as a vehicle for the development of a common understanding among subject tutors. (It should be noted that as the partnership developments were proceeding, not only were university subject tutors and teachers in school who had worked the previous model having to change their mode of operation, but there was also an influx of new colleagues joining the university staff in a period of substantial change.) The description was found to be helpful, and was also distributed to the student teachers, so that all involved in that part of their work would have a reference point in case of misunderstanding. What was not possible was the insistence that any or all of the description would be carried out, partly because it had no status apart from that of a guideline, but of course, there was no agreed contractual statement of obligation against which action could be measured.

Much then depended on the university's messages being clear and unequivocal, but the connected issue of how teachers' time and commitment in schools was to be supported was a crucial factor which interlinked with the advice and implied demands made on them. The reality was that virtually everything had to rely on teachers' goodwill, as resources beyond those of advice, exhortation and a reliance on established levels of cooperation were woefully insufficient. This situation seems to have been present elsewhere. A writer who seems to have had no knowledge of the Leicester developments wrote: 'All, however, is not rosy. There have been real problems experienced by the first cohort of mentors, mainly to do with time management, training and unclear communications' (Shaw, 1992).

A bid was made to a charitable foundation for development funding, but it was unsuccessful, and there seemed to be no immediate solution to a problem which underlined the vulnerability of all the arrangements which had gone on to date.

It is a mark of the commitment of all the then partners that in this unsatisfactory, not to say bleak, resourcing situation, the whole course did in fact move to the partnership model, with all subject groups participating from 1991. This meant a course with forty-eight partnership schools, in sixteen different clusters, involving almost 200 teachers in designated roles in the training of 220 or so student teachers.

Whereas the role of teachers in schools took a higher profile, in no way could the development of joint working with schools in the model be seen as a reduction of the university's participation. The allocation of time might have changed, but the involvement of tutors actually increased. Nearly all the university tutors involved in the secondary PGCE took on roles both as a subject tutor and a link tutor, thus increasing the level and breadth of their own participation in the course. In every sense, the participation of all partners increased and became more intense. In crude terms, everyone had to work harder to achieve the ambitious objectives of the new pattern. A fuller description of the course as it existed in 1991 will be found in Everton and White (1992).

Two developments occurred in the Summer of 1991 which addressed the issues of resources and consistency. The first of these was the university's success in its bid to the TEED (Training, Enterprise and Education Directorate) of the Department of Employment to support the Action Planning in Teacher Training project, led by David Tomley. A major part of the project was involved with initial teacher education. This enabled funds to be used in 1991–2 to support professional tutors in their part of the role of helping student teachers to review their progress and make plans for meeting negotiated targets, both within the course structure and for further professional development in the early years of their teaching career. The actual figures available to schools from this funding were minimal, but combined with a continuing modest support from the LEA, it did at least provide an earnest of the need to give financial backing in a scenario where the work-load was increasing. The LEA representatives on the Partnership Steering Group had succeeded in arranging an allocation from the funds available for teacher retention and recruitment, secure in the knowledge that the majority of newly qualified teachers in the county were in fact recruited from the ranks of those holding the university's PGCE. It was clear that no such LEA funds would be available from 1992, however. In the meantime, we began to learn some of the logistical problems which arise in the transfer of funds from one institution to another.

The second major development fundamental to the scheme's expansion to the whole course was the preparation of a common set of teaching and learning materials for the professional course, produced by university tutors for distribution to all student teachers and professional tutors. This professional topics file was a major undertaking for the editorial and production team, and the importance of their achievement cannot be overstated. It provided a common basis for link tutors and professional tutors to work from, gave a structure for the student teachers' professional coursework and, through its design, recognized the wide range of previous experience and expertise which they brought to the course. In combination with a structure of progress tutorials introduced to support the Action Planning project and a record of professional studies for student teachers to maintain, it was invaluable in giving a consistency of purpose to the link tutor and professional tutor axis upon which so much of the success of the scheme depended. The extent to which individual contributions to the scheme were precisely drawn was an issue which would become crucial when contracts as required by Circular 9/92 were written. The general level of understanding about relative roles and contributions was made easier by the professional topics file's existence, although it is recognized that there were variable interpretations of the specifics involved.

As to ensuring the quality of provision, the university was able to call on the services of its external consultant, who was a local head teacher appointed for a number of years to report independently to the university staff on the operation of the secondary PGCE. This role was additional to, but different from that undertaken by the traditional external examiners, who would make judgments on student-teacher performance and the assessment of it. The external consultant's relationship with the university was less formalized, and related to student-teacher experiences of aspects of the training, with feedback elicited through interviews with student groups. The system had been established some years before any move towards partnership, and in the new situation was considered to be a valuable indication of the reactions of student teachers to what was offered to them. Feedback from them through a disinterested party could be measured against that of previous cohorts to provide a rapid indication of whether or not hopes for the new scheme were being fulfilled. From 1989 to 1991, it was also clear from the reports that with two schemes running concurrently, there was healthy envy of whatever the other scheme provided!

It was perfectly proper too for a head teacher to be investigating student teachers' experiences within schools, and the external consultant's findings as provided in six monthly reports to the university staff were a valuable source of evidence in the steering of the developments and formulating measures for the promotion of consistency and good practice.

Parallel Developments

The introduction of the Action Planning project in 1991 had a huge impact on the working of the course but also in its development in line with the requirements of Circular 9/92. As stated above, the Leicester partnership predates the circular and in many cases the structure and implied sharing of roles does not conflict with it. One of the problems which we did find was the tuning of arrangements to fit some of the other requirements. Individual Action Planning (IAP) soon became central to the student teacher experience of the course, but was also a format which could be adapted to the new requirements regarding teacher involvement in course design and planning, and the adoption of a competence-based model of assessment.

As its introduction coincided with that of the professional topics file and the adoption of the partnership scheme for all secondary students, it was seen as a unifying structure rather than simply yet another innovation. It made enormous demands on individuals' time and energy, but the overall potential benefits were quickly recognized by most of those involved. An interim evaluation of the project, conducted by Tim Everton (Everton, 1992) and a full report written by Debbie Wall (Wall, 1993) are generally positive. For instance,

> Students also expressed satisfaction with the IAP process itself. In particular, the setting and prioritising of individual targets and goals was seen as useful to personal development throughout the course and the benefits derived in terms of personal

> organisation and time management were also acknowledged as a direct result of this. (Wall, 1993)

and

> Tutors were convinced of the value of the IAP and their support was fundamental to its integration into Secondary [. . .] courses. They were also involved with IAP development work in partnership with colleagues in schools. (Wall, 1993)

Apart from the element of action planning which was central to the professional course, each subject area was able to consider ways in which the process might be developed in their own area. In this way, a number of parallel developments took place, some involving student teachers directly, using, for example, the IAP approach while undertaking practical classroom work in schools, others choosing to work more closely with teachers in designing and developing course materials to support the student teachers' work. In both cases, not only were these developments seen as legitimate ways of being able to support schools financially for their contribution to the development, but they also furnished a mechanism for jointly addressing some of the as yet unknown requirements of Circular 9/92.

Impact of Circular 9/92

In her stimulating description of her experience of the Oxford Internship Scheme, Hake asserts 'Genuine partnership cannot be imposed by Government directions' (Hake, 1993).

The experience at Leicester showed that real partnership was the result of close working relationships between partners, a mutual confidence and trust, built up over an experience of working together, and a willingness to develop and experiment within the realities of a particular situation with local features. Circular 9/92 acknowledges none of these prerequisites, and asserts that partnerships are based on contracts, formal structures and specifications. It would be naive to deny that none of these had their place in a fully developed model wherein all partners had a secure understanding of their roles and responsibilities. Local experience had already indicated areas of the existing arrangements which were prone to strain and confusion, and where clarification and specification would be necessary. The size of the operation to a certain extent would have led naturally to the elaboration of such agreed divisions of roles as was felt to be beneficial. The immediate impact was, however, to change the nature of the agenda of discussions, and to remove the initiative from a localized basis of real negotiation about what was felt locally to be necessary to a context of compliance with an imposed set of norms which, superficially reflected much of what was going on in the Leicester scheme, but which fundamentally threatened to change the nature of the relationships between schools and the university. It was as if the initiatives which had taken so much energy and commitment to develop were hijacked by an exterior force which took no account of the real situation.

Certain of the requirements of the circular were relatively unproblematic for the Leicester course to meet. For instance, as the time student teachers spent in schools was already the equivalent of twenty-one weeks, in circumstances which already complied with the circular, it was easy to extend this to twenty-four, in advance of the required starting date. Similarly, there already was a substantial involvement of teachers in the recruitment procedures for the course, so that practice did not have to be altered. Indeed, when for financial reasons we had to reduce the level of teacher involvement, it was found that we still more than met the requirements.

Other issues were however less straightforward, and it could be claimed that such problems arose ironically from the Leicester partnership's predating of the circular. To a certain extent, it was necessary to unpick arrangements and relationships in order to meet new criteria which by their somewhat mechanistic character threatened to undermine the quality provision for which the partners had been striving.

As a first strategy, it was recognized that the Partnership Steering Group which had been formed in 1990 needed to change in constitution and remit. Its purpose had been to provide a forum for discussion and consultation, but what was now needed was a representative group with real executive power. A consultation meeting with heads and principals of existing partnership schools and colleges in the Autumn of 1992 confirmed this proposal. It was agreed that three school constituencies (head teacher, professional tutor and co-tutor) should be represented and that there should be an equal number of university tutor representatives. Elections were held through a postal ballot, with each school being entitled to cast a single vote in each constituency, and university tutor representatives were elected by their colleagues. The terms of the reference of the new Partnership Steering Committee included the responsibility to approve all changes to the course and the funding arrangements for participating schools.

The immediate resourcing problem for 1992 was met by the

provision, as part of the national pattern, of the UFC/HEFCE Transitional Funding arrangements. As predicted, the LEA was unable to sustain financial support, and the continuing modest TEED funds specifically supported the IAP project work. Over 70 per cent of the Leicester Transitional Funding allocation was transferred to schools in 1992–3, with 100 per cent of the much reduced allocation in 1993–4.

In the meantime, an advisory group to the Partnership Steering Committee set to work on establishing a proper set of funding arrangements for the continuation of the scheme. The circular specifies the need for funds to transfer from higher education institutions to schools, but leaves such arrangements for local decision. The issue was very much in the public domain, with all kinds of speculative discussion in the press and a maelstrom of unpredictable government announcements and leaks, some motivated by political ends which clearly had little to do with teacher education, about possible alternative means of funding or providing for the training of new teachers. There was a series of documents produced by bodies which represented the interests of teachers, not all of which accurately reflected local realities.

In such circumstances, it is unsurprising that participants in the negotiations sometimes felt confused. The university was also having to come to terms with a new situation, with which it felt uncomfortable, largely because of the uncertainties of the future structures of provision. The long-term implications of transferring on a continuing basis substantial funds to institutions over which it had no control was not as easily dealt with as some school colleagues first thought. Not only would it have to consider its overall role in the activity of initial teacher education, but serious questions were posed about its ability to sustain an adequate level of staff to provide for it in any case. The funding could only be spent once! On the university side, the negotiators had to learn to understand something of the real concerns of schools which had become used to working under LMS.

Nevertheless the advisory group struggled to resolve what sometimes appeared to be opposing directions in order to establish an agreed position which attempted to reflect the needs of schools and the ability of the university to provide funding over more than the immediate future. Remarkably, this was achieved, although there had been moments in the discussions when such an outcome seemed illusory.

Concurrently, the Partnership Steering Committee set itself to work jointly on addressing the other major issues contained in Circular 9/92 and the CATE note of guidance which accompanied it (CATE, 1992). A draft Institutional Development Plan was drawn up, presented to a CATE working group at a workshop in June 1993, and adopted by the

Partnership Steering Committee as the basis for further development. Taking account of the financial difficulties, and the partners' wishes to retain quality, it was quite clear that the Secretary of State's demands that all changes should be in place by 1994 was hopelessly optimistic. A phased introduction of the changes was thus decided upon, with all the partners recognizing that, whatever their stance over the desirability of such moves, such a policy was in theory at least, possible. One cannot yet determine whether this optimism is well-founded.

Neither is it possible to examine in any worthwhile sense the implications of the Institutional Development Plan, for almost as soon as this was promoted as the requirement for accreditation procedures, the procedures themselves were suspended. It was then made clear in a letter from the Secretary of State to the Committee of Vice-Chancellors and Principals (Patten, 1993) that there had been a change of policy, and that Institutional Development Plans would no longer be required as the main document for the new procedures. The reactions of those most closely concerned with the preparation of the Institutional Development Plan are probably best left to the imagination.

The story is thus incomplete. At the time of writing, we have yet to meet many of the requirements of Circular 9/92 but are working towards doing so in good faith. In some ways the forced pace of change in the most recent period has served to provide a stronger sense of working together between the partners as the elected representatives have a more highly developed sense of each other's positions. It is difficult, however, to avoid the feeling that in many other ways, the imposition of directives from outside has not resulted itself in improvement, but has rather provoked wariness in some quarters and an undesirable and unproductive insecurity among all involved in the process of educating the next generation of teachers. Bringing the financial aspects of training into the open was necessary but in some ways uncomfortable. Equally clearly the question of resources has yet to be resolved. This would have been the case whether Circular 9/92 existed or not. But the implication that somehow local arrangements can adequately deal in the long-term with a nationally controlled situation is unrealistic.

One is sometimes left to wonder if, had there not been the imperative of Circular 9/92, the developments we were already engaged in would not have led to broadly similar outcomes as those required, but retaining the goodwill of all and without the frantic timescale handed down with little apparent sense of reality from above. In optimistic moments, we can point to the continued commitment of partners and their willingness to dedicate themselves to the best possible outcome for the student teachers. At other times, we can speculate as to the level of ownership which our partners will really have if they recognize that their commitment and initiative have been hijacked.

References

CATE (1986) *Links between Initial Training Institutions and Schools* (Catenote 4) London, CATE.

CATE (1992) *The Accreditation of Initial Teacher Training under Circulars 9/92 (Department for Education) and 35/92 (Welsh Office): A note of guidance from the Council for the Accreditation of Teacher Education*, London, CATE.

DFE (1992) *Initial Teacher Training (Secondary Phase) (Circular 9/92)* London, HMSO (*Circular 35/92*) Cardiff, Welsh Office.

EVERTON, T. (1992) *Action Planning in Teacher Education: Interim Evaluation Report*, Leicester, University of Leicester School of Education.

EVERTON, T. and IMPEY, G. (Eds) (1989) *IT-INSET: Partnership in Training, The Leicestershire Experience*, London, David Fulton.

EVERTON, T. and WHITE, S. (1992) 'Partnership in training: The University of Leicester's new model of school-based teacher education', *Cambridge Journal of Education*, 22, 2, pp. 143–55.

HAKE, C. (1993) *Partnership in Initial Teacher Training: Talk and Chalk*, London, Tufnell Press.

PATTEN, J. (1993) 'Initial Teacher Training: Quality Control', Letter to Kenneth Edwards, Chair of CVCP, 30 November.

PRICE, M. (1990) *PGCE Secondary Partnership Pilot Interim Evaluation Report*, Leicester, University of Leicester School of Education.

SHAW, R. (1992) *Teacher Training in Secondary Schools*, London, Kogan Page.

SIMON, B. (1980) 'Education: The new perspective', in GORDON, P. (Ed) *The Study of Education*, 2, London, Woburn Press.

WALL, D. (1993) *Action Planning in Teacher Training (APTT) Final Evaluation Report*, Leicester, University of Leicester School of Education.

Chapter 5

Partnership: The Oxford Internship Scheme

Anna Pendry

The Oxford Internship Scheme is a school-focused secondary PGCE programme offered by the Oxford University Department of Educational Studies (OUDES) and its partnership schools. This chapter seeks to describe its genesis and initial development, the principles of the scheme and some of the ways in which the partnership between schools and the university are played out in practice. Finally, a challenge for the future is presented, in the light of seven years experience with the scheme.

The Development of Internship

Unlike many innovations in education, the introduction of internship was preceded by years of planning. Both school teachers and university tutors were involved in these processes, and account was taken of relevant research evidence, current practice and expertise in teacher education, and the realities of schooling. To be described thus, it must be an unusual innovation — it was not simply a response to political pressure, it did not ignore what was known about the processes of learning to teach, it did not deliberately ignore the perspectives of those who were to be central to its implementation. Internship represented a new approach to genuinely school-focused initial teacher education; an approach involving a real and elaborated partnership between the university, local schools and the local education authority.

In effect, planning for internship began in the mid 1970s, since the developments between then and the mid-1980s were to provide the foundations for the detailed planning that took place from 1985–7. A crucially important characteristic of those early years was the increasingly close relationship between Oxford University Department of Educational Studies and Oxfordshire LEA, and its schools. The appointment of Harry Judge, previously the head of a large state comprehensive school, as director of OUDES in 1973 was critical, and his leadership led to the designation of local schools as 'associated schools', to which all OUDES students were attached for their teaching practice. Within these schools, the role of professional tutor became increasingly important, with a senior member of staff assuming responsibility for the student's school experience in conjunction with the subject supervisor. Relationships between the university and schools were further enhanced both by the secondment of large numbers of local school teachers to the department, and by the foundation of Oxford Education Research Group. The active support and encouragement of the Chief Education Officer, Tim Brighouse, for these and other initiatives was another of the cornerstones that made internship possible.

Serious attempts to reformulate the PGCE programme began within OUDES in 1984, concurrent with but not led by Circular 3/84, but it was not until 1985 that a formal proposal was made to head teachers and LEA representatives to adopt a new model as a means of 'changing the basis of the training of graduates as teachers' (Judge, 1985). The model proposed was to provide a blueprint for the organizational features of what became internship: weeks split between school and university, blocks of time in school, concentrations of students in a relatively small number of schools, school mentors responsible for pairs of students. The director's paper ended with the words 'I believe that this is the right direction and pace at which to move. I want to go. Is anybody else coming?' (Judge, 1985). His personal commitment, charismatic presentation, the history of the previous decade and the quality of the proposals were an irresistible force: the head teachers, the authority and OUDES tutors committed themselves to the adoption of the internship model.

The LEA agreed to second twelve teachers for the following academic year to work with the tutors in the university department to develop the new model, and by February 1986 the members of the development group had been identified. However, quite what their task was to be was by no means clear, and the six months from January to July 1986 involved extensive discussion by OUDES tutors to determine what conception of teacher education would be represented by the structures that had been adopted. The role of Donald McIntyre, newly appointed as the Reader, was central in formulating the principles of the scheme, which would then be enacted through the agreed structures. These principles, expressed in inevitably abstract terms at this stage, appeared to have been accepted, at least by university staff. However, what proved to be an erroneous assumption that tacit consent was the same as acceptance and commitment, was to become all too evident in the following academic year, as the development group began its work. Insufficient attention was paid to the significance of subjective meanings of change, and a significant characteristic of the following year were to be the difficulties that emerged as tutors developed these meanings.

Each member of the group was to explore, through action research, a particular aspect of the new programme; and their work was coordinated by this author. As the year progressed, however, tension became increasingly apparent between, on the one hand the development group, its coordinator and the Reader, and on the other, other tutors within OUDES. This tension was most apparent at the regular joint meeting of OUDES staff and the development group. The purpose of these meetings was to provide a forum for discussing all aspects of the new PGCE and to make decisions related to policy. The involvement of non-departmental staff in OUDES decision-making was one of the problematic issues, but perhaps more significant was the now increasingly evident objective reality of the changes. In addition many of these realities were being expounded by school teachers, rather than university teacher educators, in what was certainly perceived (and sometimes intended) as a prescriptive and authoritarian way. There was scant sympathy for other university participants and little opportunity for them to negotiate their own meanings of change. In addition to the discomfort for tutors in hearing their own work and expertise commented on in abstract and theoretical terms by school teachers, it was also increasingly apparent that one of the real meanings of change would be a significant diminution of autonomy for university tutors. One of the desirable freedoms of higher education was being threatened and yet, in this phase of the change, what would compensate for the loss was not apparent. Despite this, progress was being made, and in January 1987 when an 'open evening' was held for all interested schools the response was overwhelmingly positive. When, in the Spring, they were asked if they would like to join the scheme the following September, offers were received in excess of the number of PGCE interns (as the students were now to be called) we had accepted.

In April, significant changes were made to the pace and nature of the development work. The director, who had been away from Oxford on sabbatical leave the previous term, returned to Oxford and initiated changes designed to ensure that all those OUDES staff who had become alienated from the development work became re-engaged, and that some of the important gaps in the programme were filled. This meant delaying the incorporation of all the theoretical understandings generated by the as yet incomplete research by the development group, and a more pragmatic definition of the tasks to be achieved in the immediate future. Whilst the development group's emphasis had undoubtedly been on the quality of change, the director's was on the involvement of all, especially permanent members of staff, and a clear route to implementation in the Autumn. The culmination of the planning year was a weekend conference in July 1987 at which all the schools to be involved were represented. The purpose of the conference was to inform and induct, and finally to launch the new programme of teacher education.

In many ways, the development of internship exemplifies the issues related to educational change discussed by Michael Fullan (Fullan, 1991). It also exemplifies them in the context of an English university, where expertise and autonomy are jealously guarded. It is doubtful if many of the painful elements of the process of change could have been avoided, but an understanding of the theory of change and the sociology of knowledge could certainly be of value to anyone engaged in change in teacher education.

The Principles of Internship

The principles of the scheme were formulated as a response to some of the problems identified as endemic to teacher education in this country. Many of these problems relate either to discontinuities between school and university or to conditions for learning in schools. Educational theorizing was often deemed as irrelevant (and it often was), there was little opportunity to try out ideas in school, little was learnt from the extensive knowledge and skills of experienced teachers, school visits from tutors were seen as occasions for survival rather than learning, students learnt to perform differently for different audiences, often colluding with their school subject supervisor on the occasion of a tutor's visit, learning was achieved through a painful process of trial and error in an unguided and non-analytical way, in an environment where students were perceived as marginal 'soft' targets.

The recognition of these sorts of problems and what could be learned from research on teaching and learning to teach was of fundamental importance in generating the principles of the scheme, principles which owe much to the work of Donald McIntyre, and he has elaborated them much more fully elsewhere (see, for example, McIntyre, 1988, 1991). The intention here is to present them in a summary form, which will then be used to indicate how the practices of internship are rooted in a theorized conception of teacher education, and not just a set of organizational arrangements.

Research into teaching has important implications for teacher education. As Donald McIntyre concluded in 1980, 'There is not, nor can there be, any systematic corpus of theoretical knowledge from which prescriptive principles for teaching can be generated.' Whilst beginners might find this superficially attractive, the nature of teaching makes it impossible. If that kind of knowledge cannot be available then the question becomes one of the nature and quality of different kinds of knowledge which could be available. McIntyre suggests that there are three major kinds, all of which should be regarded as tentative and to be tested as none of this knowledge is totally reliable or universally applicable: it should be regarded as a set of ideas to be examined and tested. Thus the findings of, for example, process–product type research are a valuable source which should not be ignored. Similarly the sophisticated thinking and skills embedded in experienced teachers' day-to-day practice, their professional craft knowledge, is another valuable source. So too is the accumulated experience and wisdom of teachers and teacher educators. Research then suggests that all of these are of potential value to the beginner but that each needs to be tested against a range of criteria, criteria as diverse as practicality, feasibility, acceptability, theoretical coherence, consistency with educational and social values, consistency with research evidence. As well as being informed by research evidence related to knowledge about teaching, the principles of internship were also influenced by research on the processes of learning to teach. This research indicates that beginner teachers have their own agenda for learning to teach: they start from their own experiences and commitments, and they will continue to do so unless we take seriously their concerns and interests. Secondly beginners will want to test out ideas for themselves. Even if prescriptions seem attractive, in reality they will be rejected as the student teacher explores the options for him/her self. Finally, this type of research also suggests that when beginners are offered the opportunity to learn in less complex and threatening environments than was often the case on 'teaching practice', then they are able to explore and develop their teaching with objectivity and rationality.

The key principles which were formulated from such findings, and which were to provide the underpinning for internship were:

- the extensive and intensive attachment of interns to one school, so that initial teacher education becomes important for the school and so that interns acquire situational knowledge and the status of junior staff membership;

- the creation of secure learning environments in which the integrated school–university curriculum is flexibly designed to ensure support and security for confident exploration of issues and problems of classroom teaching;
- the recognition that interns set their own agendas in relation to their own needs and aspirations and the need to encourage their use of a wide range of sources of ideas and insights into teaching;
- the division of labour between university and school staff, with each providing the kind of knowledge which they are best placed to provide;
- the need to test all ideas, whatever their source, against a wide range of criteria, relating to both the 'academic' and the 'practical';
- the need for progression within the programme, to reflect the interns' growing competence, and their need to both have their competence recognized and to increasingly develop their skills of self evaluation; and
- the need to locate the primary concern of classroom teaching in a contextualized study of the wider issues of schooling. (adapted from McIntyre, 1991, p. 126)

These then are the principles of internship, as they were originally formulated. What is probably most distinctive about these principles is that they use what can be learned from research to avoid or overcome what have been long-standing problems in teacher education. It cannot be claimed that these ideas always inform the practices which are adopted within the scheme, nor that they do not themselves need a critical review in the light of both experience and further research. What can be claimed is that they have proved realistic and practical, and that the model can be extremely effective in the education of highly competent practitioners who are able to examine, analyse, evaluate and develop their practice.

Partnership in Practice

Structure and organization

In the current academic year (1993–4), the internship scheme involves thirty schools as full partners, a significant increase from the original sixteen. This increase has partly resulted from a rise in student numbers at OUDES, and also the integration of many of Westminster College's secondary PGCE students within the internship programme. Hence this year there are approximately 250 interns involved in internship. These interns are normally attached to schools in subject pairs, and in each school there are normally at least four sets of pairs. The majority of schools have eight or nine interns attached to them throughout the year, but several have more. The involvement of schools is renegotiated on an annual basis, and schools need to meet the requirements of partnership which have been agreed by the Internship Partnership Committee, a group which represents head teachers, school mentors and professional tutors, the local education authority, the university and Westminster College. These requirements have been articulated in the *Guidelines for Partnership*, a deliberately non-legalistic document which indicates the respective responsibilities and roles of both schools and higher education. Schools, for example, need to offer (normally) a minimum of eight places, in subjects for which a suitable mentor is available, and be prepared to commit devolved resources to supporting the creation of time for mentors and professional tutors to fulfil their responsibilities to the interns. Clarifying the criteria for partnership and articulating them in an appropriate form is a current concern, especially as such criteria have an important role to play in ensuring that the contexts for teacher education are appropriate and that all involved are able to fulfil their responsibilities adequately.

The interns' experience in their internship year extends from the end of September until May. Before they come to Oxford they spend two orientation weeks in a primary and then secondary school near their home, and then for about thirteen weeks they spend two days a week in their internship school and three in the university — a period known as J (joint) weeks, which straddles the Christmas vacation. From the end of January until May half-term they are effectively full-time in school, during S weeks, with just occasional days back in the university. At Summer half-term they leave their internship school and then have a four-week period of alternative second-school experience, an experience not discussed in this chapter. This extensive involvement in one school, for much of the year, is fundamental to the principles of the scheme. It is this which affords the interns the opportunity to develop the complex situational knowledge they need if they are to become really effective teachers and it also enables them to become a part of the school so that they are no longer regarded (by themselves, by teachers or by pupils) as marginal visitors. The interns are able to learn about, and contribute to, the whole life of a school, in all its diversity, at different times of the year. It means that the business of teacher education is very much part of the life of the school — it is hard to ignore eight or more interns, especially when they are there for nine months.

During that year, there are two strands to the interns' programme: their subject-specific or curriculum work and the general programme which is concerned with whole-school, cross-curricular issues. The curriculum programme is the responsibility of the university curriculum tutor and school mentor, and the university general tutor and school professional tutor share responsibility for the general programme. In a number of ways basic characteristics of these two strands exemplify the principles of internship. Each is an integrated programme, in which issues explored in the university context are then pursued in school and the realities of schooling are brought back for discussion in the university context. Within these programmes, the contributions made by school and university staff are jointly planned by tutors and teachers to be different, distinctive and yet complementary so that interns gain access to the range of knowledge of value to them and to the diverse criteria against which to test that knowledge. Both programmes have progression built into them, both in terms of the demands made on the interns and in relation to the outcomes expected of them. Thus their classroom or curriculum work will begin with them working with small groups for parts of lessons, often in collaboration with an experienced teacher. Gradually, as they learn the skills of teaching, their context for learning becomes less protected as they assume greater responsibility for classes and lessons. The competences or qualities which they are expected to demonstrate are explicitly articulated in their profiling document and indicate to them both how they need to progress and the terms in which they will be assessed. As the year progresses they are increasingly expected to show not just their understanding of these qualities but their achievement of them in the classroom. The work in the general programme is also structured progressively, with a set of core questions to address all the issues they tackle. These questions begin with an emphasis on information gathering and sifting from their perspective as a beginner teacher in a school, and advance to wider questions of principle about what schools can and should do in relation to a range of issues.

Internship thus actively involves 250 interns from two higher education institutions, working in thirty schools with over 130 mentors, thirty professional tutors, at least 300 other school staff, twenty-nine curriculum tutors and thirty general tutors; all working within a single scheme of initial teacher education. Inevitably this means that issues of ensuring quality and comparability of experience for all those involved are complex. How we define quality, in relation to what, how we promote it and how we monitor and control it, are all problematic — and all need to be seriously addressed in both intellectual and practical terms.

Roles and responsibilities

The key roles in internship are those of the school mentor and the university curriculum tutor, responsible for the interns' curriculum work associated with the classroom teaching of their subject, and the school professional tutor and university general tutor, responsible for the interns' general programme work on whole-school, cross-curricular issues. These roles are fully elaborated in the *Mentor and Professional Tutor Handbook*, a document which had its genesis in the original work of the development group and which has been subsequently developed through a research project led by Hazel Hagger. It is now available in a published form (Hagger, Burn and McIntyre, 1993). The roles are designed to complement one another. Thus 'the curriculum tutor and mentor complement each other. Each has a distinctive contribution to make to the professional development of interns in relation to classroom practice' (*Handbook*, 1993, p. 19), whilst 'The professional tutor, working in partnership with the school's general tutor coordinates all activities related to internship in his/her school and together they share the planning, organisation and monitoring of the general programme for the school's interns' (op. cit., p. 21).

The mentor's role is expressed in terms of their responsibilities and these are responsibilities which derive primarily from the mentor's location within school and his or her skills as an experienced teacher. They include managing the school-based programme for the pair of interns, working collaboratively with them, observing the interns' teaching and providing feedback on it, opening up their own practice and helping interns to gain access to their own craft knowledge, helping the interns to develop the skills of self-evaluation and critically discussing the interns' own ideas. They also have a major responsibility to assess, in relation to agreed common criteria, the competence of the interns in the school setting. These are responsibilities which have at their heart the mentor's existing expertise as teacher, but they also require mentors to develop new skills as school-based teacher educators and a programme of induction and development is available for all mentors.

The curriculum tutor's responsibilities relate to leading a team of mentors in designing and evaluating the programme for all the interns in one subject area, arranging the placements of interns in schools, leading sessions in the university, supporting the interns and mentors in school and contributing to and moderating the mentors' assessment of the interns. With the mentors, curriculum tutors agree on the criteria for selection, and make selection decisions together; together they design and implement the programme; they make joint assessment decisions and together they evaluate the programme.

Similarly, the professional tutor and general tutor work as partners. Together they will plan and implement the school-based element of the general programme. There is a common general programme for all interns across schools but this will be mediated for a particular school and group of interns by the professional and general tutor. The professional tutor and his or her colleagues will contribute to this programme, which will both induct the interns into the school but also provide them with a case study for the critical examination of general issues of schooling. The professional tutor will arrange and monitor the interns' attachment to a tutor group throughout the year, and will liaise with year heads and tutors to achieve this. Professional tutors will also support and coordinate the work of mentors within the school, and provide the main channel of communication between the school and the university department in relation to the administration of the scheme. The general tutor works closely with the professional tutor in the school context but also works with the group of interns in the university, leading seminars and workshops in the common programme, sessions which are designed to complement what will be happening in the context of the individual school.

The roles and responsibilities within internship are designed to ensure that the principles can be achieved, in a realistic way. Through their mentor and curriculum tutor and their professional tutor and general tutor, interns have access to a range of types of knowledge about teaching. The roles seek to achieve a division of labour in which university and school staff offer to the interns the kind of knowledge that they are best placed to provide and which thus derives directly from their occupational position. They are designed to ensure that interns can receive coherent and integrated programmes which have support and security built into them. They are designed to ensure that the interns learn about both classroom teaching and wider issues of schooling. And that these are studied both in terms of general principles, theories and evidence as well as in relation to the specific school context in which an intern is working.

The General Programme

The general programme is concerned with whole-school, cross-curricular issues. These are currently organized into three broad themes, within which several topics are studied as exemplars of the particular theme. The three themes are 'Curriculum and Assessment', with topics on, for example, the National Curriculum, information technology and personal, social and health education; the 'Structures of Schooling', including topics on the role of the form tutor and the politics of schooling and 'Taking Account of Differences', considering specific issues such as ability, gender, race and class. In addition to these common themes, studied by all interns, there are also questions in the programme, which are related to each of the topics. These questions range from 'Where am I starting from?' i.e., establishing the interns' existing preconceptions and knowledge through to 'What can and should schools do in relation to this issue?' The programme is organized so that throughout J weeks (from September to January) there is a common session in the university once a week, which is then followed up in each of the internship schools. The university session may take the form of a presentation with a follow-up seminar in school groups; it may take the form of an extended workshop. In each case, materials are provided for both tutors and interns by nominated tutors who have expertise in any given field. The weekly school-based session will be designed to complement that offered in the university, and offers the intern a detailed case study of the topic in question, which can be subjected to critical analysis. Thus, for example, a university session on gender might examine the research evidence related to the ways in which gender is a significant issue in schooling whilst the school-based session could involve the interns in both collecting data relevant to the schools' practices (e.g., in terms of classroom interaction, the language of documentation, the displays in the school), and then talking with the school's equal opportunities coordinator to establish what the school's policy is and why it takes that form. Similarly, a university-based session on the educational and political arguments for a national curriculum and the structure and nature of the current National Curriculum might be followed in a school by an examination of the school's timetable to see how the requirements of key stages 3 and 4 have been met and what the implications are of the school's timetabling for the educational experience of the pupils. The role of the professional tutor is critical here if the interns are not simply to learn about and accept the school's policies and practices — they need to be encouraged to question those policies and practices professionally so that they can understand what they are but also see them in the light of other evidence and other possibilities. Without that, their professional development will be impoverished, and the principal outcome of the programme will be to socialize them into the culture of the school.

In S weeks (from the end of January until May), professional tutors and general tutors have more freedom to design their own individual programmes for the weekly school session, although the distinctive programmes of each internship school have to meet common criteria, and the organizing questions still need to be addressed. The criteria include revisiting some of the topics introduced earlier in the year, devoting some sessions to the concerns of the interns, ensuring that issues of particular concern in an individual school are addressed. Thus a programme might well include a session on the role of the school governors, linked to the theme on the 'Structures of Schooling', and a session led by newly qualified teachers on time management if this is of interest to the interns. In these sessions, as in J weeks, a variety of teaching methods may be adopted, ranging from seminars led by a specialist member of staff such as the head of special needs, discussions initiated by interns about their concerns, the use of case studies based on the school's practices, a role-play related to, for example, the role of the form tutor, an out-of-school visit to see the school's catchment area, an investigation and report back related to a particular aspect of schooling.

Assessment within this element of the programme is the shared responsibility of professional and general tutors. The interns' profile includes two sections of relevance to this aspect of their work: qualities of educational thinking and general professional qualities. At the three formal assessment points in the year judgments are made, following profiling conversations between each intern and those working with them. In making these judgments a wide range of different types of evidence are taken into account: the intern's contribution to discussion, their contribution to the school as a whole, their work with form tutors and other teachers and their written work.

The general programme is currently being reviewed by a joint working party of general and professional tutors. As with all aspects of internship it was originally designed collaboratively by school and university staff and increasingly all partners have recognized the need for a reappraisal of its nature and relevance and the distinctive contributions which school and university can make to this aspect of the interns' learning. Of particular concern is the overall coherence of the themes in the programme and how they can be made accessible and relevant, through appropriate pedagogy, to beginning teachers. Also of concern is the relationship between the school and university-based sessions, and achieving reasonable comparability of experience for interns in so many different schools.

The Curriculum Programme

Within the internship scheme, each curriculum area designs its own programme, with due regard to the principles of the scheme and external requirements. The subject areas offered by OUDES are English, history, geography, mathematics, modern languages and science, and Westminster offers English, modern languages and religious education. Rather than attempt to describe all the different programmes, history is offered as an example. The history programme, for the twenty-eight history interns, is designed collaboratively by the fifteen mentors and two tutors and is divided into a number of themes which are addressed throughout the year. These include such areas as history in the National Curriculum, lesson planning, classroom management, teaching strategies in history, student (i.e., pupil) understanding in history and assessment in history. Work related to each of these themes takes place both in the context of school and the university, and there is a detailed programme to show what will happen, where and why. This spells out the nature of the contribution to be made by intern, mentor and tutor, and helps to ensure a coherent and integrated programme for all the history interns in their eight different schools.

As an example, the interns' work on lesson planning attempts to ensure that they have access to a wide variety of types of knowledge and expertise about planning and diverse opportunities to develop their skills and understanding. In the university context they consider the possible functions and purposes of planning and a range of conceptual models of the nature of planning. They explore in detail one model, that of decision-making, discussing the sorts of decisions that will need to be made and the factors which could and should be taken into account in making those decisions. They have an opportunity, in an entirely safe environment, to practise the planning of real lessons, and the chance to evaluate the variety of forms that a lesson plan, or script for a lesson, might take. Finally they consider the research evidence about the nature of experienced teachers' planning, so that they can recognize what they can, and cannot learn from them. These sessions involve abstracting from the specifics to look at general principles, they make explicit what experienced teachers may take for granted, they make use of the public knowledge drawn from research which is valuable in understanding the process of planning, they provide an opportunity to scrutinize a single aspect of the skills of teaching, they emphasize issues which may not be emphasized in the context of a single school, they provide an efficient means of introducing essential ideas to a group of twenty-eight students, they allow for peer-group discussion and critique. In the school context, the interns will plan collaboratively, with their mentor, a process in which he or she will make explicit his or her skills. In that context they will only have to be responsible for a small part of the lesson, giving them the opportunity to learn without having to address all the issues relevant to a whole lesson in one go. They will teach with their mentor, in a protected environment, and then evaluate the lesson with their mentor in a way which will enable them to learn from the experience. They will plan a lesson on their own, and then review their plan with their mentor so that any problems with it can be addressed before they result in a disaster in the classroom. When they teach the lesson, the mentor is likely to be there both to support them during the lesson but also so that they can evaluate its effectiveness afterwards. They may then consider repeating that lesson, but with a class which contains a significant proportion of slower learners, and with their mentor they may consider how the lesson will need to be adapted. Increasingly, as time goes on, the interns will have more responsibility, and a less protected environment so that their skills of independent planning and teaching can develop. Thus the school context provides them with the opportunity to learn from the skills of an experienced teacher and offers them the opportunity to learn about how to make real and appropriate decisions and how to evaluate their effectiveness. It allows them the opportunity to learn how lessons need to be tailored to individual classes and pupils and offers them the opportunity to practise in a supportive and protected environment. It offers them the opportunity to test out the ideas that have been introduced in the university context, and their findings from their endeavours will be subsequently discussed in the university. Each of the themes in the programme is treated in a similar way, with specified activities and tasks in school and in the university, activities which are designed to ensure that the two contributions are different, distinctive and complementary. A key issue in relation to the school element of the programme is ensuring its feasibility in relation to the realities of schools, and this has developed with experience so that the programme is sufficiently flexible to take account of such realities and yet sufficiently prescribed to ensure coherence for the interns, and reasonable equity in their experiences. In addition to the planned programme, with its school and university tasks, there is also a deliberately unplanned element — time in the university when the unpredictable realities of schools and the interns' own concerns can be discussed and analysed as they arise.

When S weeks begin, and the interns are full-time in school, the programme becomes much more flexible, still indicating themes to be pursued over broad blocks of time, and specified occasions for reviewing progress, but located now in a context when much of the interns' time is spent working, with more or less responsibility, as beginner teachers. However, the emphasis on them as learners is maintained: this is not just the time to 'practise teaching' but also to learn about teaching and being a teacher. During the S weeks, as in J weeks, curriculum tutors will visit the interns and mentor in school to contribute to their learning. The nature of these visits is essentially determined by the mentor — he or she decides, with the interns, how the tutor can best support them. They are not assessment visits, but visits which may involve some focused lesson observation, discussion of lessons, discussion with the mentor about the interns' progress and achievements or difficulties, discussion with the mentor about the skills of mentoring. Increasingly the emphasis has been on these visits as occasions to support the mentor, rather than the interns. Thus it is the mentor's agenda that determines the focus for the visit, which normally lasts for a whole school morning.

The interns' learning during the year is seen as falling into two phases. The initial phase, usually until about the end of the Spring term, is concerned with them achieving competence in relation to the predetermined criteria of what a beginner teacher needs to be able to achieve to be described as competent: the criteria which are indicated as qualities in their profiling document. Thus they will be developing interactive teaching qualities in the classroom, qualities of educational thinking, especially in relation to the planning and evaluation of the lessons, and general professional qualities. Their work in school, in both J and S weeks, their work in the university and their written assignments all provide evidence related to these qualities. Once they are deemed to have gained essential competence, a demanding enough requirement, they then move in to phase two of the course. Here, in the last part of S weeks, the emphasis is on them developing the criteria in terms of which they, as individuals, wish to be assessed as teachers, and through the process of self-evaluation they learn how they can assess their own teaching in these terms: a process which it is hoped will help them to continue their professional development long into the future.

All the elements of the curriculum experience of the interns are designed, implemented and evaluated by mentors and tutors working collaboratively. Decisions about the nature and content of the programme are made jointly, as are decisions about the progress of individual interns. The division of responsibilities laid out in Circular 9/92 is not the model of internship — here both school and university each contribute to virtually every aspect of the interns' learning, but contribute in ways which reflect their distinctive expertise. However, achieving this is not easy; it requires time to negotiate, it requires honesty by all partners to express what they really think should be happening, it requires a genuine respect on the part of university tutors for the skills and expertise of teachers, and similarly the respect of teachers for what a university can offer. It requires each of the partners to recognize what they can, and cannot offer and it requires both mentor and tutor to recognize that their different contributions are equally valid. If one is seen as more significant or more valuable than the other, then this form of partnership is bound to break down. It depends, therefore, on a theorized understanding of the nature of teacher education.

The Future?

At this point in time it is not easy to see quite what the future holds for internship. On occasions it has been trumpeted as the flagship of the government's move towards school-based teacher education. Nothing could be less true. It is certainly a strongly school-focused programme, which puts the expertise of schools and teachers at its heart, but it also asserts the role of the university as a critical contributor to teacher education. It is not an apprenticeship scheme, nor is it a 'loony theory into practice model'. It recognizes (but does not create) the complexity of teaching and the processes of learning to teach. It recognizes that beginning teachers should have access to as many forms of knowledge and as many different types of experience as they can, provided that that knowledge and those experiences will be valuable to them in their development as future educators. But it seems that these sensible propositions are politically and ideologically unattractive. Teaching is seen as essentially simple: at most what is needed is a sound body of subject knowledge and some practice in classroom management so that that knowledge can be transmitted to the learners. What then is required is the acquisition of a relevant degree, the chance to observe and work with teachers in schools and the opportunity for practice of the not very demanding skills that have been observed.

The role for higher education, and the likes of the internship scheme is non-existent in such a scenario. An alternative, marginally less bleak future, is posited by the worst reading of Circular 9/92. Here, higher education would have some role in selecting students, an administrative role in arranging school placements, a role in monitoring the students' experience to ensure that it met external criteria, a role in ensuring that they were assessed and a role in awarding the PGCE qualification. The conception of teacher education which underlies this scenario is not so different from the first. The role of higher education is either administrative or relates to issues of quality control. But teaching is still seen as simple, the sources of knowledge from which beginner teachers can learn are either located in university subject faculties or in schools, the processes of learning to teach are not complex. Higher education has no real role to play in the education of future teachers, just in the maintenance of the system.

An alternative version of the future assumes that we have to take seriously the real financial and political context in which initial teacher education now operates, and it recognizes that there will be a wide range of different routes into teaching and that many university departments of education will need to lessen their dependence on initial teacher education. But it does not give up on the quality of the teaching profession. Instead, it asserts that universities need to maintain their contribution to the teaching of beginning teachers because they do have knowledge which is of value if teachers of the future are to be able to evaluate their practice against a range of criteria, are to be able to develop and extend their skills and understanding throughout their careers, are to be able to adapt and change. If student teachers effectively only have access to the here and now, to the inevitably and appropriately limited range of concerns that characterize the day-to-day thinking of experienced teachers, to what just one or two school contexts can offer them then they will be impoverished professionals. They certainly must have access to those things, and have the opportunity to learn as much as they can from them, but they also need access to thinking and opportunities which reveal alternative practices, alternative ways of thinking, criteria concerned with long-term goals, with issues of social justice and so on. To expect schools, without the support and involvement of higher education, to take on all those functions is to divert them from their primary purpose: that of educating their pupils. Not only does higher education have a crucial teaching function in relation to the beginner teachers themselves, but it also has an important task to do in supporting mentors and enabling them to become and continue to be effective school-based teacher educators.

The immediate task for higher education is perhaps to clarify these two roles: how it can contribute in valuable ways to the learning of beginning teachers, and how that contribution will relate to the increased contribution of school-based teacher educators. The internship scheme has already done much to conceptualize the role of mentors and others in school, and to clarify the ways in which the school-based experience must be at the heart of initial teacher education. In those terms it has broken new ground and given the word partnership real meaning. It has gone some way to identifying the distinctive university contribution and the ways in which that relates to the school contribution. But that is the challenge for the future: to argue and to demonstrate, not merely assert, the way in which universities have a valuable contribution to make to initial teacher education, a contribution which extends beyond that of administration and quality control and which reflects the idea of a university.

References

BENTON, P. (Ed) (1990) *The Oxford Internship Scheme: Integration and Partnership in Initial Teacher Education*, London, Calouste Gulbenkian Foundation.

FULLAN, M. (1991) *The New Meaning of Educational Change*, 2nd ed., London, Cassell.

HAGGER, H., BURN, K. and MCINTYRE, D. (1993) *The School Mentor Handbook*, London, Kogan Page.

JUDGE, H. (1985) 'Teachers and Professional development: A New Model June 1985', Unpublished paper, OUDES.

MCINTYRE, D. (1988) 'Designing a teacher education curriculum from research and theory on teacher knowledge', in CALDERHEAD, J. *Teachers' Professional Learning*, London, Falmer Press.

MCINTYRE, D. (1991) 'The Oxford University model of teacher education', *South Pacific Journal of Teacher Education*, 19, 2, pp. 117–29.

Chapter 6

Partnership: The Goldsmiths Experience

Sally Inman, Pat Mahony, Susan Sidgewick and Mary Stiasny

The London context of Initial Teacher Education (ITE) is very different from the situation in other parts of the country. There are thirty-four London boroughs each with their own Local Education Authority (LEA), many of which have been newly created following the abolition of the Inner London Education Authority (ILEA). There are more than a dozen Higher Education Institutions (HEIs) providing ITE courses. Therefore London HEIs are not in the situation of having a small number of LEAs with which to build up stable and close relationships over a period of time. Schools have typically related to several institutions at the same time, and HEIs have had students placed in large numbers of schools, spread over many LEAs. It is also worth noting some of the features of instability in the London context. First, changes in personnel, structures and policies in many LEAs, consequent on the abolition of the ILEA, were intensified by rate capping. Second, the comparatively high staff turnover in London schools leads to changes in the personnel involved with students. Thus in the area in which we work in South East London there are almost a dozen training institutions competing to a greater or lesser extent for links with schools. Put concretely, we have in the past worked with 200 students in eighty schools in twenty LEAs. Developing partnership in this context has been a challenging affair.

The fact that the majority of 'our' schools operate in an inner-city context influences their approach to working with student teachers. A recent report (HMI, 1991) identified the skills needed by teachers in inner-city schools, for example the ability to make provision for bilingual English learners in multicultural classrooms and the need to challenge low expectations and achievement (we would also add the need to be sensitive to children suffering disruptions caused by poverty and social dislocation). The report also pointed out that inner-city schools by and large only recruit from the pool of new teachers who have been trained in an inner-city context. Because of these factors the schools with which we work are often keen to take student teachers. They are regarded as a valuable source of new recruits and their presence in classrooms is seen positively as an extra staffing resource within an ethos of in-class support.

In recent years, and in line with the growing commitment to the principles of working on an equal and collaborative basis with schools and teachers, different sections of the college course had already been moving to establish partnership with schools and teachers. For example, the modern languages (Harris, 1993), maths and science courses were all developing forms of partnership with teachers and schools. However, the crucial factor in providing a model for partnership over the whole of the course was the successful partnership with school departments which the social studies tutors had been developing since the mid-1970s, and which had been commended by HMI (Inman and Stiasny, 1987). Thus when Circular 9/92 (DFE, 1992) was published we were in the position of being able to build on and strengthen structures and processes which we already knew worked successfully. This emphasis on the subject as the organizing focus was intensified by the coincidental fact that a large number of education tutors left the college. Thus contraction in staffing resources together with successful experiences of subject-focused partnership arrangements led to the adoption of the present scheme.

Moving Towards a Partnership Postgraduate Certificate of Education (PGCE)

In planning and putting into practice a school-based partnership PGCE course we found ourselves negotiating between three sets of imperatives.

First, there are the requirements contained in the government circular 9/92, namely that schools must play a much larger role in ITE as full partners, with students spending two-thirds of their year in schools, and that the content of courses should be driven by a profile of teacher competences.

Second, the model of partnership has been shaped by long-established principles, developed by the social studies team and which all staff (school and college-based tutors) have also wished to adopt. These were that schools should be full partners with higher education; that the relationship between school and college-based tutors should be equal and democratic; that theory and practice cannot be divorced from each other; and that the course should be founded on a model of teachers as professionals with an informed and critical understanding of the basis of their practice. As the social studies tutors argued in 1987 in discussing the partnership which they had established:

> . . . any model of teacher education that excludes teachers from key areas of the training process and in which college tutors do not themselves teach regularly in schools is educationally indefensible . . . teacher education courses which do not work in an equal partnership with schools operate to sustain and reproduce a mental/manual split in which teachers remain defined as practitioners whilst college tutors remain defined as theorists . . . (Inman and Stiasny, 1987)

We saw no problems in reconciling our principles with the requirements of circular 9/92; the two approaches are, at the least, not inconsistent with each other. However, many of the tensions which have arisen lie in trying to reconcile these principles with other contradictory messages coming from the government. It has become increasingly clear that the agenda for some policy makers is not one of equal partnership but a radical transfer of responsibility and resources for ITE to schools and the relegation of HEI to a minor or non-existent role.

These tensions are condensed into the issue of resourcing which constitutes the third set of imperatives within which we have been working and the key to what kind of course and partnership is possible. Schools and colleges have been left to strike local deals as part of a policy of generating a market in ITE which, in terms of the government's stated belief in the virtues of the free market, will lead to more 'rational' forms of school-based training which are responsive to 'real' needs. Given the conditions described earlier, London could be ripe for the outbreak of a price war between HEIs which could in turn lead to the erosion of the principles underpinning our equal partnership approach. In trying to negotiate these principles within the price this potential scenario has never been far from our minds.

From Principle to Practice

At the heart of our partnership with schools is the close working relationship between the college subject tutor and the school subject departments in which students are placed. These partnerships are self-forming in that where possible they are built on existing good working relationships between the individual members of staff concerned. Over the last eighteen months we have, with our school partners, begun to make explicit the principles on which these good relationships are based and these now serve as the public criteria against which mutual selection occurs (see Appendix 2.1).

The notion of a teaching school does not fit easily with this model of partnership because, while in some schools there may be six or seven partnerships, in others there may be only two. In many cases schools are also working with other institutions.

Two students are placed in each department. The college transfers £1,500 to the school (i.e., £750 for each student), a sum which is intended to release a teacher to work with two students for a specified period of time each week throughout the school year. Exactly how much time this payment 'buys' is an issue to which we shall return later. Resourcing is intentionally directed towards those experienced teachers who in practice work most closely with students. Within each subject area the group of college and school-based tutors is responsible for deciding who does what, where and why, in relation to the school and college-based elements of the subject course. The implementation of the partnership PGCE was phased over two years, beginning with four subject areas in September 1992 and the other six in 1993. Although its financial basis is as yet unresolved, there is also a partnership arrangement in relation to the cross-curricular elements of the course. In most schools the senior teacher responsible for students either runs, or arranges for others to run, seminars on whole-school issues. One concern here is that in schools which take students from more than one institution the senior staff encounter real problems in coordinating a school-based programme which takes account of differently patterned courses. There is a working party composed of college tutors and a group of these senior teachers whose function is to act as a steering group to advise on the new course and to plan the college and school-based cross-curricular elements of it.

For many years the social studies college and school-based tutors have agreed that this model of partnership is rich in positive potential and that benefits operate at a number of interrelated levels: either through the enhanced experiences of students and tutors or directly to the pupils themselves. These benefits are clearly echoed in preliminary reports from tutors who have been involved for the first time. In the long-run, benefits to pupils ought to be at the heart of any educational reform and as the following comments illustrate, they clearly do benefit from an improvement in the standard of teaching:

> Within Modern Languages, lessons are jointly prepared, taught and evaluated. This means that lessons are more thoroughly prepared, more lively and varied and the pupils receive more individual attention. (Anderson, 1993)

> Because the school based tutors are setting themselves very high standards in the lessons which the students are in, then it makes them question what they are offering in their other lessons. (Harris, 1993)

Our experience so far runs contrary to the popular belief that more school-based training necessarily means compromising the standard of the teaching pupils receive.

> Because we've got a carefully phased introduction to teaching, you don't get whole lessons taught badly over a period of time. I've never had so little to say about classroom management — by the time they came to the block practice students were much more competent in this respect. (Harris, 1993)

Student teachers also benefit through the increased coherence in the course brought about by college and school-based tutors working collaboratively. For one tutor this was described as the opportunity:

> to work with a group of people to develop a coherent set of experiences for students which has meant that we have got a much clearer idea of what we are trying to do. (Edwards, 1993)

For another:

> Absolutely key to it is that they're getting consistent and complementary messages. In the past students would have been working with a whole range of teachers. The mutual selection which has gone on means that as a group of tutors we all have a shared understanding of what counts as good practice. It's much harder for students to get into a downward spiral of doing badly. (Harris, 1993)

Both college and school-based tutors felt that their own professionalism had been considerably enhanced.

> I am very aware of the benefits to my own professional development in working with a group of school-based tutors who

> have, as a group, an enormous range of expertise to share. Also it's wonderful to have a sense of shared responsibility for students' development and to be able to get a picture earlier of their strengths and weaknesses. It's a whole different ball-game. (Harris, 1993)

Familiar activities, for example interviewing applicants, can become transformed when they take place collaboratively in the school.

> Yesterday we interviewed eight applicants; there were two students from this year in the school, the head of department and the second in the department and all were involved in the process. It became a professional development activity. We were in a context where we could share our basic values and philosophies. I found it really stimulating. (Edwards, 1993)

School-based tutors have similarly reported positive experiences concerning their professional practice.

> The observations of one English school-based tutor, that the new course made her feel 'more important and relevant to the students', and that it encouraged her 'to reflect on the practice in the department and the school', highlighted two responses that came up again and again through evaluations. (Moore, 1993)

School-based tutors have also reported that partnership has led them to think more reflectively about their own practice as the following two comments by school-based tutors quoted in Moore illustrate.

> It really makes you think about your own teaching practices . . . It has broadened my field of experience, provided a welcome relief from my other duties of teaching and departmental management. It has ensured that we have, as a department, been kept in close touch with a vital area of the educational process.

> By actually going through the process of teaching I have had opportunities to learn and refine my own methods. (*ibid.*)

In the following case, involvement in partnership has had beneficial consequences for the whole school department.

> It has helped raise the professionalism of the department, as all English teachers have been involved . . . It adds to the status of

> the department within the school; it has increased links with other departments taking students. (*ibid.*)

The notion of 'links with other departments' appears to be part of an emerging pattern of partnerships being formed beyond the strict requirements of the course.

> What I think is really fascinating is that partnerships are happening in different contexts. There is the partnership between college and school, partnerships between teachers, between students and between students and teachers, and where we are in partnership with more than one department in a school, there are partnerships emerging between departments. (Edwards, 1993)

All the tutors involved in the partnership PGCE this year agree that there can be enormous benefits to departments in terms of curriculum development. In social studies, for example, it has long been the practice for students' course assignments to include curriculum planning and resourcing exercises which are routinely fed back into partnership departments. In one of the schools, geography students set up a weather station, in others modern languages students undertook a variety of curriculum-development projects which again were shared across all the departments in the partnership.

It is not only individuals who benefit. Senior managers in some schools value involvement in partnership because of the role it can play in school development plans. Working with students and newly qualified teachers (NQTs) are seen as 'interrelated phases' (McDermott, 1993) within an overall policy for school-based professional development which contributes to the school becoming a 'whole-learning institution' (Farrar, 1993).

Not only do those teachers who are school-based tutors extend their professional expertise but so also do other teachers, by being invited to contribute to sessions on aspects of whole-school policy for students and NQTs. Furthermore, the skills of mentoring, for example target setting, identifying and interpreting significant elements in the structure and flow of lessons, are also fundamental to effective classroom teaching (Shaw, 1992). Mentoring directly raises the standard of classroom practice, or in Ofsted-speak, 'the standard of classroom delivery of the National Curriculum'. Because of these benefits many schools have been willing up till now, to bear some of the costs of partnership.

So far we have concentrated on the positive features emerging from the partnership PGCE at what is a very early stage in its development. It would be possible for those not directly involved in ITE to believe that our experiences this year have been managed effortlessly and the myth that school-based training leaves college tutors idle would be laughable were it not to have such serious implications. An enormous amount of time, hard work and careful thought has gone into establishing and maintaining the partnerships, organizing the development meetings and maintaining coherence in the course. In addition, it would be a mistake to think that we have stepped into a glorious, problem-free future. While the partnership scheme holds clear benefits and considerable potential for development, a number of issues have arisen which cannot be ignored.

Problems in Partnership

One issue is the question of what kinds of expertise the different partners have and how it is shared. For example, it is widely assumed that a concomitant of partnership is the provision of mentor training for the teachers involved. However, if partnership is an exercise in collaboration between equals, then teachers and tutors meet to bring their different but complementary areas of expertise together in meetings which are perhaps better described as course-development meetings. The professional development that undoubtedly occurs for the school-based tutors is generated by the fact that they are taking on new roles and responsibilities and by the way in which they share their experiences with each other. This is a very complex process which can only be developed through open discussion over time and not by attendance at a once-and-for-all 'mentor training course' where specific skills are transmitted. As tutors have said:

> mentor training is not a one-off but an ongoing process . . . it should not be conceived as a one way process in which we train the mentors to train the students but as a reciprocal training process in which both sides have much to learn. (see Appendix 2.2)

It is for this reason that we have stretched the payment to schools over the school year which runs beyond the time when students are on course. For one tutor this tension was expressed as:

> What we're involved in are processes not events. Yet there's an enormous bureaucratic pressure to prove that you've 'done your

> mentor training'. It's difficult to make publicly explicit just what's involved but it's certainly not just a matter of a few training sessions either for me or the school based tutors. (Edwards, 1993)

As Edwards hints, the complex process of sharing expertise involves a shift in professional identity for the college tutor. This is not without its stresses. Some tutors have reported experiencing considerable anxiety while they analyse and make explicit the nature of their expertise in relation to that of the teachers with whom they work.

The collaborative nature of the partnership can also create tensions as well as opportunities. In one case a school-based tutor left the school mid-year having gained promotion. The school suggested another tutor who turned out to be unable to fulfil the requirements. This raised a number of difficult questions such as who chooses the school-based tutor and how the different levels of partnership (the institutional and the subject-specific) can be dovetailed. In the past, when a placement broke down the student would merely have moved to another school, but in this case the partnership agreement had already been signed by both institutions and resources transferred. A relatively high staff turnover is a feature of London schools and it is likely that school-based tutors, given their positioning within the career structure, will apply for and gain promotion. It is not easy to see how HEIs could properly discharge their responsibility for quality of courses were they to have no control over the appointment of staff working with the students. As one tutor put it:

> At what point do you say they're part of a team and need support and encouragement and at what point do you say enough is enough — it's too damaging for the students. What you do when you've said that, is really difficult, you're right in the middle of school politics.

Similar issues occur the other way round of course and it should not be assumed that schools are always satisfied with the quality of provision from the college side of the partnership. Here too there are similar sensitivities about 'telling tales' within line-management structures. What we conclude from all this is the huge importance of human relationships in partnership schemes. Official documentation often gives the impression that the relationship between schools and HEIs consists of nothing more than quasi-legal agreements monitored and controlled by bureaucratic means. Nothing could be further from the truth. A high-quality provision for student teachers rests on the quality of professional relationships between the partners and these are not built overnight. As the social studies tutors said:

> . . . our own experiences of initiating and running a school-based course have made us acutely aware that the development of an 'equal partnership' with schools in the training of teachers is a lengthy and complex process which necessitates a commitment on the part of college tutors and teachers at a 'grass roots' as well as an institutional level. This remains as pertinent now as it was when we began. (Inman and Stiasny, 1987)

From Principle to Price

Unsurprisingly, the issues of resourcing and the logistics of student numbers continue to be the main source of concern. By extending the formal involvement of school teachers the cost of the course is massively increased with no concomitant rise in income, in a context where teachers are having to take on many other initiatives, and where HEI and many schools are suffering budget cuts.

The issue of funding is of great concern to schools and there has been considerable negotiation over what constitutes reasonable funding for the school's involvement. The sum of £1,500 was originally intended to fund a main-scale teacher to release the school-based tutor to work with the students for half a day per week throughout the year. This figure was suggested by the steering group when negotiations started two years ago. During those two years, because of increased salary costs and pressures on school budgets, the amount of time thus bought has had to be reduced, with obvious implications for the role of the school-based tutor. Lest it be thought that the solution is to transfer more money to schools, let us consider the economics of what student fees 'buy' in terms of school and college teaching and other inputs into the course.

Of the total income brought in by each student about two-fifths go towards the cental costs of the institution. This covers not only necessary administrative functions such as medical and criminal record checks, student welfare services, examination and validation costs, but also provision of library, computer and other resource facilities necessary to the support of students' independent study. A further fifth goes towards funding about thirty-six hours of formal teaching from the school-based tutor. Finally two-fifths goes towards 240 hours of college-based tutoring. Thus for twice the cost, the student receives seven times the quantity (*sic*) of formal teaching in college compared with school. The reason for this is the highly intensive staff–student ratio required by school-based work where one tutor is working with only two students. It is no answer to increase the staff–student ratio in school, since no subject department could provide for all the school-based work of say fifteen students. Or if they could, it would only be by dint of running the equivalent of the college seminar and then placing students in other school departments for teaching practice. This sounds remarkably like the old style split between theory and practice of which the profession itself has been so critical. Here we are not arguing that centralized provision is inappropriate, on the contrary. The economies of scale possible in centralized provision enable teaching resources to be deployed in a range of different but equally effective and necessary ways (Sidgwick, Mahony and Hextall, 1993). The point is that decisions about what should be taught, where, by whom and to what size of student group must depend on what we want students to learn and not on crude assertions about the primacy of one site over another.

The profession needs urgently to engage in a debate about the purposes of teacher education. We must be able to articulate what kind of teachers we want and why, what professional characteristics and qualities teachers must possess, what learning experiences are needed for their development and how school-based and centralized provision can be integrated to provide for these in a coherent framework. Only if the profession reaches and adopts a collective stance on these issues can it plan for a preparation for teaching which is informed by reason rather than the *ad hoc* contingencies of policy motivated both by ideological antipathy and a market place driven by price rather than principle.

References

ANDERSON, J. (1993) 'Working with student teachers in the classroom: A partnership model for school based work', in *Language Learning Journal*.

DFE (1992) *Initial Teacher Training (Secondary Phase) (Circular 9/92)*, London, HMSO.

EDWARDS, G. (1993) Personal Interview.

FARRAR, M. (1993) Personal Interview.

HARRIS, V. (1993) Personal Interview.

HARRIS, V. (1993) 'Partners are people', in THOROGOOD, J. (Ed) *Aspects of Partnership*, London, Centre for Information on Language Teaching and Research.

HMI (1991) *Training Teachers for Inner City Schools*, London, HMSO.

INMAN, S. and STIASNY, M. (1987) 'Good practice in teacher education', *Educational Studies Monograph*, 3, London, Goldsmiths Publications Service.

MOORE, A. (1993) 'Finding strength through partnership: The development of a new PGCE English course', *English and Media Magazine*, 28.

MCDERMOTT, D. (1993) Personal Interview.

SHAW, R. (1992) 'Can mentoring raise achievement in schools?', in WILKIN, M. (Ed) *Mentoring in Schools*, Kogan Page.

SIDGWICK, S., MAHONY, P. and HEXTALL, I. (1993) 'Policy and practice in the professional development of teachers', in *International Studies in Sociology of Education*, 3, 11.

Chapter 7

Roles and Responsibilities in Initial Teacher Training — Student Views

Anne Williams

Introduction

The immediate future of secondary initial teacher training is yet to be finally decided although the Secretary of State has stated his intention to continue its reform (DFE, 1993). Higher education-led partnership, or joint-venture schemes are to continue and an increase in school-led courses is expected. The balance between these two forms of provision is not yet known. The Open University is entering the field of initial teacher training for the first time, offering part-time training from 1994 to both primary and secondary prospective teachers. At the time of writing, licensed teacher schemes continue to offer a route to Qualified Teacher Status (QTS) for a small number of teachers. Those who wish to become teachers therefore have an increasing choice of routes from which to choose. Some will not involve higher education at all, a route favoured by political activists (O'Hear, 1988) and pressure groups such as the Centre for Policy Studies (Lawlor, 1990). Others (Hargreaves, 1989; Barber, 1993) see a role for higher education, but not one which necessarily involves its staff directly in teaching or tutoring the student teacher. Elsewhere, genuine partnerships have been forged, such as those between schools and the university within the Oxford internship scheme, although much of the cost has, in the past, been borne by the LEA rather than by the university.

Much of the current debate in teacher education has focused upon the roles and relative responsibilities of the school and the higher education institution or other agency. An equally important partner, particularly in a system which claims to give significance to the wishes of the client, is the student whose views have not been canvassed widely. Such evidence that is available (Furlong, 1990; Williams *et al.*, 1992; Booth, 1993,) suggests that while students wish to spend a significant part of their training in school, they do see institution-based work as important and they also value the contribution of both tutors and teachers to their development as teachers. Moreover Williams *et al.*'s study suggests that the higher education tutor role is a potentially important one, not only for the work undertaken in the higher education institution, but also for the distinctive contribution which the tutor can make in supporting the student in school. This raises the question of whether, and to what extent, the higher education tutor role could be transferred to the teacher, given a resolution of issues of resources.

Williams *et al.*'s survey of students who had previously followed one PGCE course just prior to the publication of Circular 9/92, suggests that the contribution of the higher education tutor was one which would not be replicated easily by a member of the school staff. This does imply good student–tutor relationships and raises the question of whether all institutional course structures facilitate the development of such relationships.

Booth's study was also of students following a single PGCE course. His findings underlined the crucial importance of the mentor in the development of the student teachers' professional skills. He concludes that simply placing students in school without adequate mentoring support would give students little opportunity to develop effective classroom and teaching skills and understanding. While stressing the need for the full involvement of mentors in all aspects of the planning teaching and review of the course he does not address the question of whether this would be sufficient to guarantee high-quality support for students.

Earlier work by Furlong (1990) concluded that while students wanted a training which was clearly practical whether this took place at school or in the higher education institution, practice was not seen as sufficient on its own. Students also felt that they needed opportunities for reflection and for sharing and discussing their experience with others.

This chapter will discuss some of the issues of concern to students, using as illustration, information gained from interviews with students carried out at the end of their PGCE course.[1] The students were from four different higher education institutions. Thirty students were interviewed using a semi-structured interview schedule. Interviews were recorded for later transcription. Three recordings were damaged and could not be transcribed. Information from twenty-seven students is therefore used here. Questions covered a wide range of topics, including the kinds of support given by tutors and teachers and perceptions of the optimum balance between school-based and other work.

The sample consisted of seventeen female and ten male students. They were training to teach a range of secondary subjects: science (4), mathematics (3), PE (5), English (7), history (2), humanities (2), modern languages (2), technology (2). Most had been placed in comprehensive schools for their major teaching practice, although one had been in an independent school and one in a selective school. Twelve of the schools catered for the 11–18 age range, twelve for 11–16, one for 10–14, one for 11–14 and one for 14–18.

Student Views of Teacher and Tutor Support

McIntyre and Hagger (1992) have described a number of mentoring models with respect to teachers working with students in schools. Their model is also used to analyse teacher perceptions of their role as mentors by Williams (Williams, 1993). An important issue raised by the students interviewed here was the role played by the teacher and the tutor in courses where both were involved in supporting them during school placements. When asked about the sorts of support received they reported considerable variation from both tutors and teachers. At one extreme the thoroughness of the support given by teachers was exemplary, particularly since the interviews were carried out prior to the implementation of the requirements of Circular 9/92. The student received both written and oral feedback, was involved in negotiating the focus of teacher observations and had regular meetings with the teacher to discuss progress.

> Everything very detailed, she'd sit at the back and make detailed notes to say the least . . . Written and oral because I had a meeting once a week with J to discuss the actual teaching side of it and talk about any problems I had. It was very two-way — she's always there for me to talk to about something . . . She made up this actual sheet that I filled in the front page of before the observation telling her things that I'd like her to look out for and also she referred to things she made a comment about beforehand . . . so she's very detailed. (PN)

In contrast, other students felt that teachers had no time to help them and that they were on their own in school.

> I didn't really feel that I was supported in the right way, although maybe I should have asked for it more, but I also got the feeling in the school that when I did ask for anything, they were always in a rush and doing something else. (TN)

Many teachers were valued for the immediacy of their support and for their help in coping in a particular school.

> The school people could tell me the experiences they had of the children and how the work that I was doing was supposed to fit into the whole scheme of the children's education in that school because they were at the school, they knew the ethos of the school. (KB)

While a number of students received written feedback from teachers on lessons taught, many received only verbal feedback and little of any sort once the teacher was satisfied that the student was not at risk of failure. These teachers, according to the students, saw their role as checking that nothing was going badly wrong rather than as furthering the student's development as a teacher. This raises important issues about the training needed to change the teachers' perception of their role and to give them the skills needed to extend it.

> Basically their job was to oversee you and to just look at you and basically there wasn't a lot of feedback. (JB)

> I think he saw he was there basically to make sure nobody fell out of the window or that nothing really dreadful happened . . . X was lovely but he didn't like to criticize basically and I would have liked him to. (YN)

Most students did receive some feedback, either oral or written, and there were many comments about the positive nature of this.

> They'd always talk to me afterwards about it . . . it was always very positive. All the teachers I worked with, I was very lucky, they gave you really positive feedback. Not that they overpraised you and didn't tell you what your faults were, they just didn't do it in a way that undermined you at all. (SN)

While support from tutors was consistent in that it was always in the form of some written comment, in other ways, it was as variable as that provided by schools. The major difference was that while teacher support seemed to be a function of individual schools and not related to the higher education institution attended by the student, tutor support did appear to be affected by the nature of the institution. The findings reported here do raise questions about the relationship between institutional structures and tutor support. Course structures vary considerably both between different types of course, and within one type. What emerged from this limited study was that tutor support appeared to be viewed much more positively by those students who were following courses where school-based support was undertaken by the same person who taught or tutored the student in the university and where the tutor knew both the student and the school well. Several students in this situation compared tutor support favourably with that provided by teachers. This might be expected given that students were following courses prior to the implementation of partnership agreements and transfer of resources for student support.

> Well it was more structured — there was more feedback basically. I mean every lesson they watched there was more kind of talk about lesson content, lesson plans, teaching styles, so it was very structured in the way they looked at it. (JB)

> I found feedback from the tutors very helpful. To start with it was written feedback which was very thorough and looked at aspects that perhaps the head of department was missing. It was comments on paper, it wasn't just given and off you go, it was then a discussion as well. (HB)

This was not, however, the experience of all students. Some found tutor expectations unrealistic.

> I thought in some cases they were unrealistic. It seemed to me they wanted an all-singing, all-dancing sort of lesson far more concerned with the children being in groups and doing role-play and acting things . . . You give them what you know they want to see. (ML)

For others the feedback was rushed or non-existent.

> Mainly similar to the school's in that the tutor was in a hurry to be elsewhere and I had further lessons to go to so mainly it was a written report which I digested in my own time. (OL)

Where students were visited by tutors whom they felt that they did not know, their perceptions tended to be that the value of the tutor visit was much diminished. It could be argued that, where this is the case, there is little point in continued tutor visits during placements.

> In education study it says you've got to have a really good rapport with the students cos then they learn and feel confident and then they put you in with a TP tutor that you've never seen before. (PL)

At best, tutor support was seen very favourably. This depended less on the frequency of the tutors' visits than on the rapport established between tutor and students and on the quality of the feedback given.

> Well he was brilliant. I mean even though he was only here three times. He knew the school well and he knew what X was like. He would write at least one and a half side of notes for you to keep and cover certain points like management, resources etc. rapport with the children. And he was always interested in how you were getting on . . . I felt he was never intrusive and he was willing to appreciate that each school was different and something you might have tried at some other school would just not have worked at Y because say of the physical confines of the school. (YN)

When asked whether input from both teachers and tutors was needed during school practice, it became clear from the responses of these students that, given certain conditions, both were valued. The results of this study support the findings of Williams *et al.*'s survey of students who had previously followed one PGCE course just prior to the publication of Circular 9/92. This suggested that the contribution of the higher education tutor was one which would not be replicated easily by a member of the school staff. Key factors for the students who felt this were the objectivity of the tutor with no affiliation to a specific school, the breadth of school experience which some tutors can bring and the availability of someone for whom the student rather than the school is the main priority. This does imply the good student–tutor relationships referred to earlier.

The students interviewed here reinforced these views. The best tutors brought qualities which would not be replicated easily in schools, or, at least, not in all schools. The breadth of experience which tutors can bring to student support, as a result of their work in many different schools with many different pupils, students and teachers, would not be found among all, or even many, teachers. This breadth of experience is often undervalued by those who criticize the higher education input to initial teacher training, but it existed very clearly for those students who had enjoyed high-quality support.

> A different view because the teachers know what they were doing within school and how the school system worked and X is pointing out 'You've done that in school, how do you think that would apply to some of the other schools that you've been to?' (GB)

> I think it's best it shouldn't be interchangeable because your tutor should have built up a body of experience of handling students in so many different schools and situations. He or she should be very knowledgeable about the leading edge of teaching ideas, resources for their subject . . . indeed one of the values that every school I've been into has [been that they have] said 'Ah good we'll be able to get some new ideas.' (FB)

The fact that a student would not necessarily choose to teach in the same kind of school as that used for a placement was another reason advanced in support of access to a tutor who could offer several perspectives on aspects of teaching.

> I think they were offering me a very focused look at the way I taught within their school. The things I would have to improve upon to be a good teacher in their school, in that kind of environment which I decided by half-term was not the sort of environment I wanted to teach in . . . on the other hand what P could give was a more objective look at me as a teacher. I mean in that particular school but also how I'd fare in different sorts of schools. (QN)

Detachment from the specific school context is another feature of tutor support which may not be easy to achieve in all schools. The greater the commitment of the teacher to his or her pupils, the harder it is to remain objective about the student's performance with them.

> You do really need independent support because you're still very much of a guest and you feel even if you may not be, you feel very much at the mercy of the school and at the goodwill of the staff. (OL)

Tutors were also seen as needed in case of personality clashes in the school. These could be between student and school staff in which case an independent outsider may be able to help, or, in extreme cases, intervene to ensure that the student is not disadvantaged. Tensions can also arise within departments, particularly where the mentor is not the head of department and the student may need help in coping with the school politics involved.

> You can't guarantee that you're gonna get on with everyone and you could quite easily be placed with someone you don't get on with or in a department where your ideas don't work. (SN)

All of these reasons for needing both teachers and tutors assumed a good relationship between student and tutor and what the students saw as up to date and well-informed tutors. The statements quoted above were also seen as reasons for having tutor support in addition to, rather than instead of, teacher support. A minority of this group had not had this experience and for them, tutors were seen as either out of touch or not sufficiently well-known to the student to be of any help.

> I think the teachers to be honest are in a better position because obviously they know the class and they're in the classroom themselves so they really know what's what as it were. So I think that was more important than what the tutors had to say . . . Well yeah they've been sitting in their little office for the last ten years or whatever and they don't have a clue what goes on in the classroom. (ZN)

> Well to be honest with a tutor that's never seen you that doesn't really know you, has no information on you, doesn't make any effort to know you, comes in twice, can't really see the point in that to be honest. (AL)

Even here, students felt that if someone were having major problems it would require a tutor to sort out the difficulties.

> No, forget the tutors, just the teachers . . . I don't need the tutors. No everything was there in the school for me. Someone who was having bigger problems would need their tutors certainly coz there's no way teachers in schools can give up time to cope with students. (BL)

Variability of student experience is a function of a range of factors. There are, and always will be, a wide variety of schools both in terms of school type — comprehensive, selective, CTC, independent and so on, catchment, inner-city, rural, outer suburban, multi and mono cultural, ethos and level of resourcing. This is, of course, an argument for experience of more than one school, but all students will inevitably be attached to a single school for their final or major placement or to a lead or base school in school-led training and it is this school which is likely to have the greatest influence upon their immediate development as a teacher. Student experience will remain very varied in this sense. It could be argued that access to someone outside the school who can help the student to put their specific experience into context will still be needed, especially where students are likely to seek employment nationally rather than locally.

It might be argued that once resources are allocated to schools for student support, variations in levels of support will diminish. In practice however, support is a function of interest and commitment on the part of school staff (Wildman *et al.*, 1992) as well as resourcing. The students interviewed here had received support which varied both in amount and quality. In terms of the levels of mentoring described by McIntyre and Hagger (1992) and Williams (1993) some students here had experienced very minimal mentoring while in other cases, systems appeared to be well developed. Further work will need to be undertaken to monitor the effect which resource transfer and mentor preparation have upon the experience of students. There may be very positive effects upon the mentor's awareness of what is involved in this role and upon ability to undertake specific mentoring tasks. However, the extent to which training and resources will affect the priority which mentors give to their work with students compared with their other responsibilities remains an important issue, particularly where schools have taken on a major training role.

A number of the roles identified by these students were being undertaken by teachers in some instances and by tutors in others. Clearly many of these could be undertaken by teachers in all schools given training and resources. Other roles do not lend themselves so easily to this kind of interchangeability. All students felt that the support of weak students would have to involve higher education because of the time needed. This was thought necessary even if schools were better resourced for supporting students. It is related to the school's inability to guarantee priority treatment to students because their prime responsibility has to be to pupils. This priority is a major reason for retaining higher education involvement. Many students clearly felt extremely vulnerable when placed in schools and saw the reassurance which could be provided by an impartial outsider as invaluable.

At the same time, there are clearly areas of support which are much better provided by the school and which are not easily undertaken by tutors. Detailed knowledge of classes and individual pupils and of the day-to-day working of specific schools are clearly areas where the student looks first to the teacher for help. Teachers are seen as being essential to an understanding of how to teach successfully in their own school and as providers of immediate practical assistance or ideas. For other students, poor quality support from tutors means that the school has to become the major source of help.

This raises questions about the value of tutor support if tutors are assigned to students who they do not know well and are visiting schools which they do not know and where they are not known. The tutor needed to be sensitive to what might or might not work in a specific school and to be able to consider the implications for practice in different schools of a student's experience in their placement school. He or she also needed to be perceived as both up to date and realistic. Some tutors achieved all of these and their support was valued highly by students. The value of tutor support where these conditions cannot be provided seems to be questionable. In particular, tutor support which is 'bought-in' by higher education institutions may, unless carefully set up, be of little value and less useful than the support provided within the school.

Do Students Need Time at the University?

Earlier work by Furlong (1990) concluded that while students wanted a training which was clearly practical whether this took place at school or in the higher education institution, practice was not seen as sufficient on its own. Students also felt that they needed opportunities for reflection and for sharing and discussing their experience with others. Like the students described by Furlong, those described in this study all felt that they wanted to spend a lot of time in school and that they wanted a lot of practical 'hands-on' experience. They did, nevertheless, value university-based work for a variety of reasons. For a number, 'university-based' was interpreted as involving the tutors and thus included work which included school-based elements. For example, many students had been into school at a very early stage in their course to teach small groups of pupils, or parts of a lesson which had been prepared with their tutor and which was subsequently reviewed with that tutor. For some a higher education-based preparation was seen as important in order to ensure that student needs were met prior to embarking on school-based work.

> People coming on the course have lots of different backgrounds and certain areas, they just wouldn't feel confident at all, like going in to school and being faced with children or even preparing lessons at an early stage and you need a little bit of back-up and a bit of support early on at the university . . . I don't think teachers have the time . . . I think if they did it would detract from the job they're supposed to be doing . . . (HB)

> You couldn't put it all into the school because although on teaching practice your head of department was there for everything that went wrong whilst you're there, there is no way that she's got time to try to prepare you to teach, she can't give you practices in everything you're likely to come across, but the university does. It goes through teaching styles with you, through potential discipline problems, they look at equal opps . . . all that the secondary school teacher hasn't got time to do. (GB)

For others the supported introduction to work with pupils, with time available for a tutor to help students both before and after lessons was seen as valuable.

> I think the government's right in saying that you learn very quickly in front of classes and there is no substitute for spending that time in front of classes, but I think that it can be overdone. I think what we do here . . . which is small-group teaching practice, there's a lovely introduction, it's safe, it's interesting, the kids are very well resourced in small groups like that — the schools love having us. . . . (FB)

For others, the prospect of starting in school without some university-based introduction was simply seen as too stressful. Moreover it was recognized as enabling schools to benefit from work with students.

> I think that I would have found that very, very stressful and very very nerve-wracking . . . I don't know. I think I would have gone in with absolutely no experience whatsoever and there'd be nowhere to draw from. I think that would have been extremely difficult. I couldn't imagine doing that. Not even with good support within the school . . . I think you can have good

> support but with how busy teachers are I don't think you'll ever be able to have the amount of time you will need if you're going to have it totally school-based. (AB)

In some cases students felt the need for time at the university because their practice school had offered very limited support.

> I think it really stinks. Because basically student teachers are a necessary pain in the neck aren't they? You need them because you need to give people time in the school to fail or succeed and that's basically all it is . . . (PL)

In others the issue was not one of lack of support or commitment on the part of the school, but one of the ability of the school to meet the needs of all students, rather than simply those of the competent.

> I think I learned more on teaching practice than I did in my time at university. But something's got to be done to try and structure it well because otherwise I think you're just gonna lose so many people just through the net, because teachers don't have the time . . . with me here the teachers just didn't have the time to spend with me. They admitted they were glad that I was quite sort of self-sufficient and independent . . . (ML)

Some students also felt that teachers are not trained to be teacher trainers and that they should not be expected to take on this role in addition to their main job as teachers of children. For many students, someone for whom they are the priority is very important to their development and it is difficult to see how this could be provided within the school.

> I think you do need a lot of time outside the classroom to do the theory, to think about issues in schools before you go in. I mean if someone had told me to go into school in September and teach within a few weeks and just have the odd day here and there I don't think I'd have fared very well and I wouldn't have had a good impression of school and I don't think it's fair on the schools . . . I mean they've got a job to do — they've got to provide education for those children. They're not trained as teacher trainers. They might be very good mentors but they're not actually trained to do that and it's not really where their duties should lie. (QN)

These students felt that the training of teachers was a different job needing different skills and aptitudes from those required to teach children successfully.

> I think it's a real shame. I feel that for a start, the teachers aren't trained to train teachers in that way. I mean obviously to train teachers you have to have an amount of experience but then a certain sort of person becomes a tutor because they want to be involved in that and I feel that if training goes into school a lot of teachers will be landed with training students when they have no desire to be involved in training. They might have interests elsewhere no matter how wonderful they are as a trainer and I think that may cause resentment. (VN)

For several, time was needed at the university, not just because of tutor support, but for the opportunity offered to share experiences and to learn from other students.

> I found the times at university have been very useful. Being able to discuss, being able to look at issues have helped . . . I certainly enjoyed spending time in university and spending time talking with other people who're going to become teachers. (AL)

> There are all sorts of issues about sharing experiences between other students that are out at different schools, different placements . . . (FB)

Consistency of Experience

The students interviewed here were concerned about the variability of experience dependent upon the school in which they were placed. They saw this as an important factor to be considered if schools are to be given total or a major responsibility for student training.

> There must be tremendous variation between the quality and standards of schools out there which makes me worry a little when students are placed with a particular school you may get tremendous variations of standards of training. (OL)

They were equally aware of, and concerned about, the variable nature of the support given. Some were very conscious that their peers seemed to have been better supported than they were.

> I have seen a couple of reports written on my friends and seen some of the things that they've written — I thought, yeah . . . I'd like that . . . I saw one report where the teacher actually wrote down timings and things and actually wrote something, yes moved onto this part, you introduced this part well but perhaps you could have said this or you could have done that and actually to through the whole structure of what we're doing which I think would have been a benefit even if only done once. I just felt I wasn't really given anything that I could work on. (NL)

A number of students were sceptical about schools' ability to solve the problem of how to give them the time they needed and to which they felt they should be entitled. They were very conscious both of the time pressures on teachers and of the fact that their priority had to be the pupils. They were not being critical, but pointed out that teachers' conditions of service currently mean that pupils must have first call on their time, and that this has to affect ability to give guarantees of time commitments.

> I was actually talking to a teacher yesterday and she said 'How on earth am I going to fit this into my timetable and be able to give adequate time to students?' Whereas here, when my tutor comes in to see me he knows that he has this hour and a half and it's my time and nobody is gonna be able to say 'Oh, can you come — so and so's fallen and broken their leg'. I think that the thing is in a school you never know what's gonna happen from day to day whereas that time with a university tutor can be so structured. (YN)

The key point here seems to be that students need someone to be there for them, for whom they are the first priority. Some students will succeed without this support but for others it will be crucial. It can be provided by a tutor, but it should not be assumed that all tutors currently provide this level of support which depends upon good tutor–student relationships and a tutor timetable which allows for sufficient time to be set aside for the student when the school is visited. It can be provided by the school, but only if someone is charged with that specific responsibility and enabled to make it a priority.

Conclusion

Initial teacher training is a complex undertaking, which currently takes place in varied contexts which provide different levels of training. A continued supply of well-prepared and committed new teachers depends upon provision of training which meets their needs. For some of this group of students, the school and higher education institution each had much to offer which was of value. For others, the contribution of one of the partners was seen to be less than satisfactory. It seems that, at best, both school and higher education are valued. For some students this may be necessary to their survival during what, for many, is a stressful period of training. It appears that it would be difficult for either partner to assume fully the role currently played by the other. If this is the case, then ways need to be found which enable both to continue to play a full part in teacher training, while allowing other forms of provision to develop to meet the needs of different students. This means identifying not only those conditions in school which are best able to ensure good support for students, but also higher education structures which provide support which is of value. The students quoted here seem to confirm that greater involvement of schools makes the management and control of quality more difficult. This is partly a question of resources which will not be solved wholly by allocating more money to schools for the training of teacher, but is also a question of priorities. Higher education may be able to offer quality guarantees not simply through being given this responsibility, but by discharging it through a continued involvement in the training process rather than simply through its management. Such a level of involvement would clearly meet the needs of many of the students interviewed here.

Note

1 The author would like to acknowledge the assistance of Mairead Dunne who conducted many of the interviews on which this chapter is based.

References

Barber, M. (1993) 'The truth about partnership', *Journal of Education for Teaching*, 19, 3, pp. 255–62.

Booth, M. (1993) 'The effectiveness and role of the mentor in school: The students' view', *Cambridge Journal of Education*, 23, 2, pp. 184–97.

DFE (1992) *Initial Teacher Training (Secondary Phase) (Circular 9/92)*, London, HMSO.

DFE (1993) *The Government's Proposals for the Reform of Initial Teacher Training*, London, HMSO.

HARGREAVES, D. (1989) *The Times Educational Supplement*, 8 September, p. 22.

HEFCE (1993) *Initial Teacher Training Allocations for 1993–4*, Bristol, HEFCE.

FURLONG, J. (1990) 'School-based training: The students views', in BOOTH, M., FURLONG, J. and WILKIN, M. (1990) *Partnership in Initial Teacher Training*, Lewes, Falmer Press.

LAWLOR, S. (1990) *Teachers Mistaught — Training in Theories or Education in Subjects?*, London, Centre for Policy Studies.

MCINTYRE, D. and HAGGER, H. (1992) 'Teachers' expertise and models of mentoring', in MCINTYRE, D., HAGGER, H. and WILKIN, M. (Eds) *Mentoring in Schools*, London, Kogan Page.

O'HEAR, A. (1988) *Who Teaches the Teachers?*, London, Social Affairs Unit.

WILDMAN, T.M., MAGLIARO, S.G., NILES, R.A. and NILES, J.A. (1992) 'Teacher mentoring: An analysis of roles, activities and conditions', *Journal of Teacher Education*, 43, 3, pp. 205–13.

WILLIAMS, E.A. (1993) 'Teacher perceptions of their needs as mentors in the context of developing school-based initial teacher education', *British Educational Research Journal*, 19, 4, pp. 407–20.

WILLIAMS, E.A., BUTT, G.W. and SOARES, A. (1992) 'Student perceptions of a secondary postgraduate certificate in education course', *Journal of Education for Teaching*, 18, 3, pp. 297–310.

Chapter 8

Partnership — A Headteacher's View

Barbara Wynn

The Role of the School

The role of the school in initial teacher education has already changed a great deal and is likely to develop further over the next few years. Many different types of partnership have developed. Some schools still have a very traditional role where they provide placements for, and reports on, students and very little else. If any such scheme is called a partnership it is one with very unequal partners for the university or college takes all the major decisions with little consultation. The students themselves may be launched straight into the classroom with very little help or guidance after the first few lessons. Other schools, perhaps encouraged by the financial support available, or the lack of teacher-training institutions in their area have decided to take over the training of teachers either on their own or as part of a consortium. The majority of schools are likely to take a middle road in building a partnership with colleges and universities. Whether the finances rest with the initial training institution or are held by the schools who then buy in time and support from the university, the principles of partnership are of vital importance.

Partnership

The true partnership approach has many advantages. When it works well it should give the students the best of both worlds. They will have a great dèal of time in, and support from, the schools, but they will also be able to reflect on what they have seen with the help of lecturers who are not based in the same institution. They will have opportunities to compare notes with other students and to develop their own perspectives.

From the school point of view of the type of partnership developed in the Oxfordshire Internship Scheme (discussed in Chapter 6) has many advantages. The school staff are treated as experts in their field, they are involved in the planning of the programme for the students and in the assessment of their progress at every stage. Because there are ten to twelve students in each school there is a general tutor from the university assigned to each school and he or she will come into the school most weeks to help with planning and execution of the general programme of school-based talks, tutorials and activities.

As far as possible this programme is planned to coordinate with the more intensive lectures and discussions which are taking place in the university. For example, small-scale investigations of learning support in the school will follow introductory sessions in the university and will be followed up by analysis and discussion of findings in the school. It is not intended however, that the university should provide the theory and the school show how theory can be put into practice. Theoretical and practical aspects of each issue are explored both in the initial training institution and in the school and there is a strong emphasis on critical learning. The students are expected to learn then to try out ideas and to develop as a result. Self-assessment is encouraged throughout the course. This is of course entirely appropriate as these approaches to learning are the ones which good schools encourage in their pupils.

Commitment

Schools which develop teacher-training partnerships in this way have soon found that this involvement necessitates a whole-school commitment if it is to succeed. It is essential that everyone in the school is aware of the main principles as well as the practical details. Every possible opportunity to raise relevant issues through meetings with those who are most actively involved, brief presentations at whole-staff meetings and even briefer explanations on paper will need to be given when such a scheme is introduced. This explanation will also need to be followed up at regular intervals to ensure that new staff are involved and that colleagues are aware of changes and developments which are taking place from time to time.

It is surprising how many people are directly involved in the development of new members of the profession through such a scheme. In a school with ten students there will normally be at least five subject mentors who will have a major role to play in the success of the scheme. The school needs to have a senior member of staff who oversees the work of everyone else involved and there are likely to be at least ten, possibly more staff who will talk to the interns or students about their work in the school, or even better, run activity-based sessions for them. As well as their mentors, students need to have some lesson time observing and teaching with other colleagues. This will involve at least ten more teachers. It is important that students are involved in the pastoral system of the school, perhaps with more than one year group and through this work another ten teachers and probably at least three heads of year or house will become involved. The head teacher will no doubt run an introductory session for students about the school and will want to stay in touch with what is happening. This adds up to forty teachers who are involved one way or another and although there may well be some overlap in the categories mentioned above it is equally possible that a larger number of people are involved in some schools. Responsibilities of those involved need to be clearly defined.

The Pattern of the Year

The pattern of the year will vary from one teacher-training institution to another but students are often expected to carry out a period of observation in either primary or secondary schools before they start their course. An induction to the course and to the school where they are to be placed will come next, then in some schemes, the students spend part of the week in their schools and part in the university. In others there will be arrangements for blocks of time to be spent in the school. There are many advantages of a gradual introduction to teaching both from the point of view of the student and the school. It gives the student the opportunity to be involved with school life throughout the year, and this involvement has proved to be invaluable in helping students to understand how schools work. Students can be introduced to aspects of teaching rather than being 'thrown in at the deep end' — always a doubtful method of encouraging excellence.

In the Oxfordshire scheme the students are asked to provide a self-evaluation of a part of their teaching. This involves reading about a particular aspect of their work, then evaluating their progress with the help of others, such as the student with whom they are paired and their mentor. This is an excellent way of encouraging teachers to be reflective and to improve their teaching. For example, an English student might look closely at his or her teaching of poetry. A science student might consider development of investigations and either of them might look at questioning techniques or group work. At some point the students will be ready to work on their own with classes. The mentor will advise on this change, which is likely to happen well before students are working full-time in the school.

In some partnerships the students stay in one school for most of the year, in others they work in two schools either on a part-time basis or as a second block. There are advantages and disadvantages to both systems. Staying in one school for most of the year enables students to really understand school life and become fully involved, whilst having a second school for a longer practice provides more to have a linked scheme between two schools so that there is both continuity and variety.

Academic Requirements

Schools are going to need to help students with their academic work if this involves any research of investigation within the school. This can be used to the advantage of the school which might encourage students to look at a problem which they want to investigate anyway. A school might well benefit from a small-scale research project on one aspect of its development plan, such as the reality of equal opportunity, bullying, the option system or the image of the school. Schools will obviously need to be very wary about questionnaires and interviews and to check up very carefully on these before students are allowed to use them.

Matters for the Schools' Senior Management

Planning

Although detailed timetable planning will probably be done by the subject mentor in conjunction with the university, the senior teacher overseeing the scheme, needs to help mentors with their time allocation, ensure that there is consistency between departments and organize meetings for mentors in school so that they can support one another and share good practice. He or she is likely to be responsible for the school induction programme which will need to be carefully thought out. Another responsibility is liaising with the timetabler to ensure that if the scheme allows for a session in school where all the students work together (and this would seem to be a basic requirement) that the professional tutor is available at this time.

The planning of a programme for students in school can be very satisfying professionally for the senior teacher. Involvement of one's colleagues in running activity sessions, talks, discussions and other work for students provides numerous staff-development possibilities, particularly if colleagues can be encouraged to run sessions using good teaching techniques which can serve to set a good example to the students and help them develop their own teaching style.

Although no pupil should have too much time with students it should be remembered that pupils often enjoy their work with student teachers and gain a lot from their enthusiasm, hard work and their recent studies. Senior staff will need to devise a way of monitoring the 'diet' for individual pupils, perhaps through tutors or heads of year if the timetable does not lend itself to easy analysis.

Implementation

Attention to detail is very important in the success of school-based teacher training, especially if it involves a large number of students being in a school at the same time. Staffroom conventions need to be explained and understood and space needs to be available for sitting, pigeon holes, and work areas. In many schools this is quite a problem as space is short anyway. Arrangements for coffee and lunches need to be made and the students need to be introduced to the office staff and given clear rules on photocopying and the production of resources.

Obviously anticipation of, and action to avoid, disasters is preferable to dealing with things that have gone wrong but this is a counsel of perfection and a senior teacher will often be the trouble-shooter dealing with issues for both staff and students, so close liaison is bound to be needed.

One area of induction to school life which is often done badly is to the role of the form tutor. Mentors will probably be receiving training from the university or college so that they offer the best possible support for students in the classroom but the school will probably be left to work out its own scheme for form tutors with very little guidance. Teachers need clear guidelines about what they need to do to help students to develop into good form tutors, they should certainly not be sitting in the staffroom while the student marks the register and chats to the pupils!

Monitoring and Evaluation

The senior teacher is likely to assist mentors with the observation of students, monitoring their progress and at the appropriate stage, assessing them. This can often be quite difficult for the mentor, especially if he or she has developed a very supportive approach to the student, so the help of someone who is involved but detached can be invaluable. In cases where there is a disagreement between the mentor and the university about the competence of a student, the senior teacher can again be helpful.

Communication

The senior teacher will be responsible for communication in several different directions including communication with all the teaching staff and head teacher, links with the university including regular visits from the university's main or general tutor and visits from university curriculum or subject tutors. There will need to be an agreed entitlement to visits from university tutors and it is important that the senior teacher is informed in advance of these visits so that liaison can be arranged if needed. There is nothing more infuriating than the senior teacher having to contact a university tutor about some matter, only to discover that he or she was in school earlier that day. However, with thought and good planning most problems can be avoided.

Matters for the Mentor to Consider

The role of the mentor is considered in more detail in Chapter 10 but some points are relevant in the context of a general consideration of school-based teacher training. The opportunities for staff development afforded by being a mentor are enormous. Mentors will be involved in planning, which will develop their skills and help them to understand aspects of the whole school which might well be new to them. They will be coaching, encouraging, discussing professional practice with, and assessing, students.

All these skills will be helpful to teachers who want to take on more responsibility in the future, which is one reason why many schools encourage staff who are not heads of department to take on the role of mentor once the scheme has been established. In addition to the staff-development possibilities discussed above the mentor will be having many of his or her lessons observed by students and this is likely to mean that the teaching will be well done in order to set a good example. All teachers can benefit from reviewing and reflecting on their teaching in this way.

The mentor will be responsible for some elements of planning, implementation and monitoring and assessment as outlined below.

Planning

Induction to the department and the briefing of other teachers who will be working with the students are two vital stages in school-based training and these will need to be well planned. Timetable planning is also likely to create problems as there will be a number of conflicting demands. The university is likely to ask for a certain percentage of the time to be allocated to different headings such as time with the mentor, time with other teachers, time working with a partner if the scheme involves pairing students, and time working on their own. Matching these demands to a timetable and ensuring that pupils do not have too many lessons taught by students is tricky and some flexibility will be needed. The university should provide clear guidelines and planning aids to help mentors with this task.

Implementation

A school-based teacher training partnership provides an excellent opportunity for a structured introduction to teaching. Small group work, extension work for able students, working on a limited task and evaluation of different aspects of teaching, such as successful starts to lessons can all be introduced in a controlled way. The main aim of, and satisfaction gained from, being a mentor is helping students to become competent teachers. However, it is the case that teachers who are very good at developing the talents of children do not automatically transfer their skills to the teaching of adults. Both the senior teacher and the university staff will need to be aware of this and provide help if necessary. It is important that the mentor also encourages interns to reflect upon teaching and to develop their own effective teaching style.

Monitoring and Assessment

As far as assessment is concerned the emphasis will be as agreed by the partners in teacher education but each assessment needs to have a specific focus and, as explained above, assisted self-assessment is very important. In the early days of the Oxford scheme, students were given 'chartered' status if they had reached a certain standard by a certain date. This proved to be counter-productive as those who had not quite made it felt discouraged and some of those who had attained this status then coasted. The students now pass through certain phases when they have reached a required standard. Guidelines are given on dates so that problems can be picked up and dealt with at an early stage. Although the final decision is not taken until late in the course, the assessment scheme ensures that there are regular warnings of difficulties.

In-service Needs

In school there is a need for meetings of mentors and within departments. These meetings will be better if the university has briefed mentors and senior staff well. There is a strong case for university-based meetings of professional tutors, senior teachers, mentors and occasionally of head teachers so that all are informed about the scheme. The university needs to ensure that its own staff are well briefed and enthusiastic about school-based training, as a university tutor who does not sell the programme well will harm it considerably.

Funding and Use of Money

At present most training institutions, including the Open University, hold funds and allocate some of these to schools. One vital use of this money is the provision of time for mentors to do their work. Even if the training institution is not paying the full cost of school-based training some contribution will be made and the best use of this money is for staff time. Paying individual staff more can be quite divisive and it would be difficult to allocate money fairly if the training works well and involves a large number of staff. One danger of money being allocated directly to schools may be the temptation for schools to keep the money, thinking that they know best, rather than developing a partnership with higher education to offer the students a variety of perspectives. The narrowness of this approach will not show itself for some time. In addition the problems of recruitment, assessment and time required to do what is not the primary purpose of schools are all important considerations.

The costing of the time allowed for training can be calculated. For example a school with a thirty-period week of which a standard-scale teacher teaches twenty-six periods and which allows five mentors and a senior teacher two periods a week each would spend $\frac{12}{26}$ × the cost of a teacher's salary including on-costs.

If the salary is charged at £25,000 then the time allocated costs the school £11,500. When paper, duplicating costs and office time are added the total might be £12,000, that is, £1,200 per student. Costs can be reduced by allocating less time.

It is unrealistic to expect the training institution to cover the whole of this cost, after all schools have for many years helped to train students without any financial assistance, but it is important to be able to calculate the true costs so that the benefits for staff development, good training of new colleagues and the extra input into the school can be balanced against them.

Unless the school has plenty of space the problem of overcrowding and competition for resources may be another cost, this is another reason why the whole school should be informed about, and hopefully convinced of, the merits of school-based training.

Conclusion

A full partnership between schools and higher education seems to provide the ideal system for the training and professional development of new teachers as well as offering tremendous opportunities for both school and staff development. Provided that the scheme is well planned and that the partnership works in practice as well as in name everyone should benefit.

An additional benefit of school-based training is the skills that it provides to many teachers for induction of new staff. This important process can be greatly enhanced by the use of methods used for initial training. Recruitment and retention of staff can also be enhanced both through keeping students who have trained in the school and the establishment of good methods of staff induction and development.

Chapter 9

The Role of the Higher Education Tutor

Graham Butt

> Of course school teachers are capable of delivering all aspects of initial training, just as college tutors are capable of teaching school pupils; it does not follow that because we can, therefore we ought. Our concern should be to organise the components of the courses in such a way as to secure the best possible training for students (McManus, 1993).

Introduction

There can be no doubt that following Circular 9/92 (DFE, 1992) the role of the HE tutor in training student teachers has changed dramatically. This becomes clear when one considers that Higher Education Institutions (HEIs) are now only legally responsible for 'academic validation, presenting courses for accreditation, awarding qualifications to successful students, and arranging student placements in more than one school' (par. 14, 9/92). With at least two-thirds of each student teacher's time to be spent in schools HE tutors will find that the style, if not the substance, of their work will change.

Putting aside for the moment some of the broader political reasons why the government is keen to reform Initial Teacher Education (ITE), the DFE has made clear statements about the new structures for training teachers. ITE courses are to be made more 'practical', to focus on 'teaching competences' and involve schools in a greater degree of 'partnership'. The concern expressed by HEIs though is that these 'changes' are based upon very little evidence of their previous omission from existing ITE courses. The implication that the 'traditional' routes into teaching were dangerously flawed is strongly countered.

HMI reports (1982, 1987 and 1993) on the training of new teachers plainly state that the majority of ITE courses are effective in producing highly competent classroom practitioners. Indeed the 1993 report reveals that 89 per cent of new teachers viewed their courses positively and considered them to be an adequate training for their first teaching post (69 per cent of secondary trainees refered to their ITE as either 'good' or 'very good').

Recent research has also shown that many beginning teachers do not perceive ITE as being dominated by too much 'theory'. The study by Williams *et al.* (1992) reveals that although students were not uncritical of some of the theory they received, they actually requested more time to be spent on it in certain areas of their courses.

Perhaps of greatest interest, however, is the evidence that the precursor of the 9/92 reforms, namely the Articled Teacher scheme, has not yet proved to be a more efficient model for training teachers (OHMCI, 1993a, see also p. 5).

The emphasis on greater partnership between schools and HE institutions in training teachers is the key to ITE reforms. The concept of partnership is certainly not new, although it is unfortunate that it is often narrowly equated with 'school-based' models of training first adopted by departments of education at Oxford, Sussex and the Roehampton Institute. Few HEIs would argue against moves towards developing greater partnership, but they are eager to ensure that this does not simply involve handing over training responsibilities from the HE tutor to the mentor in school. As Edwards (1992) states 'a strong HE contribution is critically important for the status and practice of teaching', whilst the necessity to establish a sound academic base in education for student teachers is equally clear.

One strength of 9/92 is that the roles adopted by both teacher and tutor in the training of students have become more openly debated. Recognition that ITE extends beyond a basic model of schools merely 'minding' students on teaching practice, or of tutors simply providing them with useless educational 'theory', may take some time — particularly if governmental and New Right commentators remain so casually blinkered to the function and purpose of ITE. However, for those observers who are more objective and equivocal this debate has prompted a worthwhile reappraisal of individual responsibilities within the training process.

The fundamental question though must be to consider the most appropriate kinds of training new entrants into the teaching profession require. The purpose of this chapter is to explore the role of the HE tutor in meeting these requirements under the direction of Circular 9/92. Whilst the majority of the comments contained here concentrate upon secondary PGCE (one-year) courses they may also be of

Figure 9.1: The Higher Education Tutor

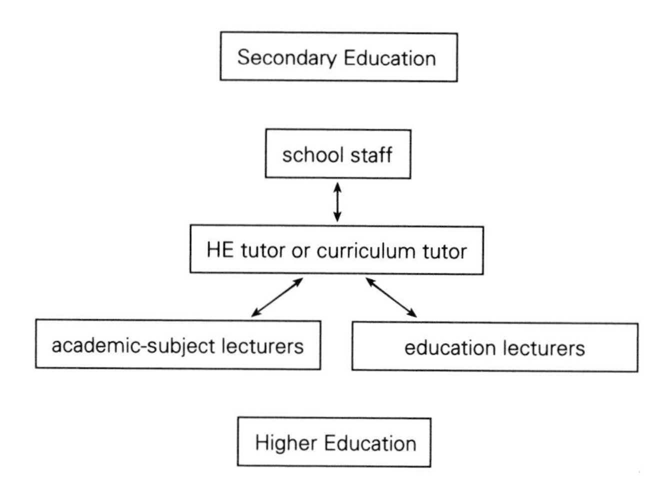

Source: Hones, 1992

relevance to the secondary Bachelor of Education degree and two-year PGCE courses.

The Role of the HE Tutor Before Circular 9/92

It is perhaps worthwhile to explore the nature of the HE tutors' commitments before Circular 9/92. The HE tutor has traditionally played a pivotal role in the education and training of new teachers by virtue of being in the middle of a 'triangle' made up by school staff, academic subject lecturers and other education lecturers (see Figure 9.1).

Hones (1992) acknowledges both the unique position and the diversity of responsibility of HE tutors through his preference for referring to them as 'curriculum tutors'; a term which illustrates a broader role than merely delivering 'method' work.

Each of the three major links in the triangle requires the HE tutor to adopt a variety of working styles. The nature of the HE tutors' position being effectively 'half way' between schools and higher education establishments has always made the job of the HE tutor different from any other individual within the triangular structure.

HE tutors have traditionally worked 'in' and 'with' schools, but also have wide-ranging commitments to their university or college. Within HE they often have less time available for research than their academic colleagues, and view their subject from fundamentally different perspectives than those of academic subject lecturers (or indeed school teachers). They are also in a special position to help facilitate curriculum development for schools (often through their work on professional bodies or subject associations), provide INSET, and contribute to the work of examination boards. With the demise of the LEAs many HE tutors have additionally found themselves under pressure to deliver different forms of professional development in schools. The role of advisory teacher is, in some localities, effectively devolving to the HE tutor.

We must remember that HE tutors are employed by an institution which sees their job as involving much more than just training new teachers. Typical job specifications for tutors list their responsibilities as teaching, researching, publishing, carrying out administrative duties for the institution, and being involved in the delivery of higher-degree work (often at BPhil Ed, MEd, MPhil and PhD level). Additionally because HE tutors have come from teaching posts within schools, and not solely through an avenue of research like other academic lecturers, there will be pressure in some institutions to research for a PhD if the tutor does not already possess one.

The link between academic-subject lecturers and other education lecturers in higher education is an interesting one. With regard to ITE the HE tutor has to decide to what extent the changing philosophy, concepts, techniques, and skills within their academic subject, or particular educational field, should be transferred onto the student teachers. It is, of course, important that someone in the training process maintains a broad and contemporary appreciation of the changes occurring in the whole educational scene. Traditionally this role has fallen to the HE tutor by virtue of his or her position at the interface between higher education and schools.

The connection between the HE tutor and staff in schools is perhaps the most crucial link in the triangle. Teachers rightly expect HE tutors not only to be experienced classroom teachers, but also to be familiar with the current educational practice, legislation in education and the daily challenges of teaching. Relationships between the tutor and the teacher must be strong if the student teacher is to benefit from the breadth of experience of both parties.

In the past, as Hones (1992) suggests, teachers may have felt that tutors in teacher education 'were too far removed from the real world, able to be unrealistic in their consideration of educational issues . . . rarely facing the need to put their ideas into actual practice'. One aspect of this tension arises from the HE tutors' stated role of research into education — a role which some teachers may feel is irrelevant. Research may not be 'accepted' by schools if the topic is considered to be either esoteric or remote from daily school experience. Additionally the role of researcher may reinforce the stereotype of the tutor being distanced from school experience and in a theoretical isolation of academic self-indulgence. However, few would argue that research and publication are vital if the professional status of education is to be maintained. It is also highly significant that HEIs are partly funded on their research performances and that many keenly protect their national research ratings. If we recognize the importance of educational research we may consider that HE tutors are the people most suited to embed this into the practice of training students.

Hones' (1992) diagram of the roles of the HE tutor has one major omission, that of the position of the student teacher within the triangular structure. This is considered in the next section.

The Changing Role of the HE Tutor

So how will the traditional roles of the HE tutor change? Tutors will now be devising their courses with teachers, rather than merely informing teachers of what the courses contain and the roles they should adopt during the supervision of students. Course handbooks will be jointly written, the selection of students will be carried out both by school and HE staff, and profiling systems for student teachers will be jointly devised and administered. A major change may be seen in the amount of time that tutors spend in supervising students on teaching practice(s) in schools. Depending on how the structure of the ITE course has evolved there may be a significant reduction in contact time between tutor and student during such practice. Many tutors feel uneasy about this lack of 'continuity' in their work and will either visit students more than the prescribed minimum, or encourage the creation of 'review periods' of contact either within the training institution or at a mutually convenient location.

Even before 9/92 the responsibilities for the tasks outlined above were often already largely shared between the school and HEI under existing partnership arrangements. What is now significant is that the whole concept of this partnership has grown. School-based elements of courses will increase (even though in most institutions school-based work accounted for 60–65 per cent of student time already) and the leading responsibility for training students 'to teach their specialist subjects, to assess pupils and to manage classes; and for supervising students and assessing their competence in these respects' (par. 14,

9/92) will lie with the schools. Wilkin (1992b) highlights an immediate tension, for 'As students are placed in schools for a higher proportion of the training period, [the HEIs'] control of the quality of training is clearly threatened' (p. 320).

With a maximum of twelve weeks devoted to the HEI-based elements of training there is a danger that blocks of student time are being allocated to schools without a full appreciation of what the students will be doing during this time. The responsibilities of HE tutors and teacher mentors during school-based work have to be fully understood and agreed upon. More time in schools does not automatically mean better training, or a mere extension of the schools' traditional role of supervising and assessing TP performance (DES/HMI, 1991; Barrett *et al.*, 1992). It is simplistic to assume that by merely increasing their allocation of 'school-based' time students will automatically become better teachers. 'Practice makes perfect' is a convenient adage, but inadequate for a process as involved and complicated as learning to teach. In many respects additional contact time with children may mean that students receive more practice at failing to cope with certain classes of disaffected children. This is clearly damaging to the student teacher and should perhaps be replaced by a reduction in practice and an increase in counselling from either an HE tutor or mentor. Being in schools for longer periods will certainly help students learn practical tips, tricks and coping strategies; but this is not all there is to being an effective and professional teacher.

The experience that student teachers gain in schools should not be devalued. Such experience is obviously fundamentally important and is rightly considered to be so by students (Williams *et al.*, 1992). Beginning teachers have a high regard for those schools that support them well, and the tutors and teachers who regularly feedback objective observations and comments. However, the OHMCI (1993c) report on the 'New Teacher in School' illustrates that some students' experiences during school placements are bleak. They may endure teaching practices with little variety of schools and few opportunities to observe good teachers or classes. The element of lottery here is worrying — the quality of the students' experience within school tends to depend mostly on the chance of being assigned to a good-quality teacher. 'These teachers will assume particular importance once the school based element of initial training is increased' (p. 32) (OHMCI, 1993c).

The traditional role of the HE tutor should therefore assume a greater importance during teaching practice. Although schools will have the leading responsibility for student supervision the HE tutor, with a broad experience of a range of schools, subject departments, students and children, can provide a vital moderating viewpoint. The distinctive contribution of the HE tutor becomes more clearly focused. As well as coordinating practice the tutor can provide a broad perspective on the subject taught, an appreciation of academic and theoretical frameworks, and an illustration of different teaching methods, materials, and strategies.

Too much school practice without the regular opportunity to discuss issues with other students and a 'detached' HE tutor will not provide a good introduction to teaching. Effective student teachers are those that feel supported, successful, confident and in control. These qualities do not result from being thrown into complex school structures and relationships without a means of periodically breaking away from the 'unremitting reality' of schools; a reality which very experienced teachers often find difficulty in coping with. As one maths student in Williams *et al*'.s (1992) research states 'Although the school I was placed in was very supportive the regular contact with university tutors and fellow trainees allowed much more opportunity to discuss experiences, to share ideas and to seek advice.'

Here then is a crucial role for the HE tutor. To provide different perspectives on educational practice, to suggest various teaching approaches, and to bring a breadth of experiences to bear on the students' successes and failures. The tutor must be able to listen and encourage, as well as promote self-criticism and reflection within the student.

It is often the HE tutor, slightly distanced from the immediacy of the classroom but aware of classroom practice and research findings, who can assist the student teacher best here. For many student teachers the HE tutor can provide an important alternative to the mores of the classroom or staffroom, a break from the unique and often parochial experience of the TP school.

Who Should Supervise the Student Teacher?

The previous section helped to illustrate some of the complementary roles of the tutor and mentor; however, the processes by which student teachers should be supervised during their time in school are still left largely unresolved by Circular 9/92. Certain government sources, and right-wing pressure groups, have been vocal about their beliefs of who should carry this responsibility. Lawlor (1992), for example, talks of young teachers being 'sent to learn' from more senior teachers who have dedicated themselves to a lifetime of imparting knowledge; whilst Beardon *et al.* (1992) also sees the role of the experienced teacher as that of sole mentor imparting the skills of subject application. O'Hear (1988) adopts an uncomplicated model of teaching, and indeed teacher training, where knowledge and skills are simply 'passed down' from above. The complex factors of understanding how children learn, of student teachers converting their degree knowledge to suitable content for children, of pedagogy, language, pastoral roles, etc. are all largely ignored in his analysis.

But can we assume that teacher mentors working alone will necessarily train and supervise student teachers better than they would in concert with HE tutors? This idea that successful teachers of children are also naturally going to be successful teachers of students is somewhat questionable, for the expertise required to train students is very different from that needed to teach children. As McIntyre (1990b) states 'being a good classroom teacher does not imply that one will be skilled at assessing the teaching of beginners, at discussing their teaching with them, or at giving them appropriate guidance' (p. 21). Future teacher mentors will obviously need to be well chosen, well trained and suitably motivated if they are to successfully educate beginning teachers. Alternatively the HE tutor still has a major role to play in the supervision and guidance of students.

The present roles of teacher and tutor in preparing students to teach has been explored by a number of writers. Furlong *et al.* (1988) have identified levels of support for the student from the HEI and school, although this analysis has been criticized by McIntyre (1990a) for its implication of a hierarchy of support with teachers occupying the lower levels. The whole concept of levels is seen as flawed, for the training of student teachers requires different forms of professional knowledge and experience rather than 'layers' of input. In effect the Oxford Internship Scheme rejects hierarchical levelling and has a variety of professional tutors, mentors, curriculum tutors and general tutors from schools and university with complementary status and input. This approach acknowledges that learning to teach is so complex that it can not be 'levelled', compartmentalized or delivered through the actions of one 'key' individual.

The HMI survey of school-based training (1991) showed that the active involvement of an HE tutor in supporting school-based work is an essential element. Underlying this assertion is the fact that the main purpose of schools is to teach pupils, not to train students. (It must be noted however, as Beardon *et al.* (1992) do, that the use of HMI reports to 'defend' ITE creates certain difficulties. Right-wing groups, for example, see them as merely representing a further indication of the educational establishment's resistance to change.)

In some cases students have rightly argued that the support of the HE tutor has been unnecessary due to the excellent guidance given by teachers. In other situations students would not have survived their teaching practice without tutor support. This obviously has much to do with the individual school, the student and the type of HE tutor and teacher in support. It again raises the issue of priority of purpose. A teacher's leading priority is to teach children — a fact made even more apparent by teacher appraisal and the publication of 'league tables' of test results which increase the pressure on teachers to concentrate on pupil attainment. Parents similarly expect that the priorities of teachers will be firmly placed with their children. It is difficult therefore to see the student teacher ever becoming a higher priority than the pupil in the work of the classroom teacher or mentor.

A factor that has often been forgotten in the future training of teachers is that of time. It is narrowly assumed that more time in schools will mean that students receive more time from teacher mentors. This may prove to be too simplistic an analysis. Williams *et al.* (1992) have revealed that many students feel that they did not receive their full entitlement of time from their supervisory teachers on teaching practice. Student teachers do not tend to 'push' these demands as they are generally sensitive to the time constraints that teachers are working under, and realize the primacy of their concern for children. This is not a problem that can be solved simply by providing more student time in schools or extra resources — the real problem is again one of priorities. Back and Booth (1992) echo this point when they note the difficulties teachers face being responsible for both children and student teachers at the same time.

Lastly the choice of which school would be most suitable for the training of students is something that experienced HE tutors, who have developed a detailed understanding of a range of different schools' subject departments within the local region, can perhaps overview best. By the nature of their contact with a large, often expanding, number of departments where students could be placed tutors normally have a sound overview of the advantages and challenges of training within different schools. Few other professionals within education develop a similar appreciation during the course of their work.

Assessment of Student Teachers

The focus for the assessment of student teachers will, in many partnerships, become the specified teaching competences. We have yet to discover the performance levels that will be required to pass these competences, or indeed their relative 'weightings'. Ellis (1993) points out that they can only be 'general guidelines to the outcomes of training' (p. 129) although the three main areas for assessment (namely effective teaching, securing effective learning and managing pupil behaviour) are clear. The competences (DFE, 1992) specifically relate to 'Subject Knowledge' (2.2), 'Subject Application' (2.3), 'Class Management' (2.4), 'Assessment and Recording of Pupils' Progress' (2.5) and 'Further Professional Development' (2.6); however, many HE tutors and teachers will have a wider conception of 'good teaching' than these competences outline. Although schools may have the lead responsibility for delivering many of these competences there are certainly aspects of their content that subject teachers will not be wholly enthusiastic about covering — both in terms of time commitment and appreciation of all the issues involved. Here the HE tutor, who will have previously introduced many of these themes in method work, has a significant role to play. This role becomes more difficult if the tutor has not regularly seen the student teacher teach during teaching practice.

The HE tutor will also be well placed to set and assess the written work of student teachers on a variety of theoretical and practical themes, and will have an important 'moderating' role with respect to teaching performance. The writing of references and student profiling will continue to be a shared responsibility and should remain so.

Despite the overarching concordance of roles amongst the HEIs and schools there does appear to be something of a division of leading responsibilities emerging. The HE tutor seems well placed to advise students using a breadth of experience of a number of schools, appreciation of the subject taught, and knowledge of research and curriculum innovation; whereas the school teacher is in the best position to inform students about teaching in a specific school, with particular groups of children.

Uniting 'Theory' and 'Practice' in ITE — The Central Role of the HE Tutor?

Antipathy towards the promotion of so called 'educational theory' by New-Right groups (including the Centre for Policy Studies, Hillgate Group, and Adam Smith Institute) has been vehement in recent years. These groups suggest that educational theory is academically worthless and distracts beginning teachers from the very task of learning to teach children. Thus, it is argued, by increasing the 'practical' school-based time in training, the irrelevancies of theory (and by implication the tutors who purvey it) will be reduced.

This ignores the change in the nature of 'theory' taught in HEIs over the past twenty-five years. Substantial movement towards a 'reflective practitioner' approach (which three-quarters of HEIs use according to the MOTE survey (Barrett *et al.*, 1992)), rather than simply learning 'theory' in the HEIs and then trying it out in 'practice' in the classroom, is barely recognized by the New Right. Learning to teach is now seen by most HEIs as a process of interpreting, analysing and explaining practice, with student teachers creating their own 'teaching theories' and reflecting upon them after school-based experience. This is clearly a very different concept of 'theory' and 'practice' as understood by the New Right, as both are 'inextricably bound up in one another' (Smith, 1992).

Kirkham (1992) illustrates the dangers of divorcing theory from practice and in so doing restates the importance of the HE tutors' contribution to the training process: 'If theoretical studies are relegated to a few essays in an otherwise entirely practical course, or if teaching becomes simply a craft to be picked up in a particular school without reference to research, then the education of pupils will become narrow and inflexible.'

Interestingly, students themselves offer the view that the balance between theory and practice in ITE is sound, as are the links between schools and HEIs. Those newly qualified teachers who criticize their training as being too theoretical rarely advance specific examples to illustrate these perceived weaknesses. Indeed some change their appreciation of theory once they start to teach (OHMCI, 1993c).

Although HE tutors have a perceived 'weak spot' amongst certain government circles and teachers regarding their distance from the 'real' experience of the classroom the actual evidence for this is somewhat limited. Many HE tutors do still teach in schools, albeit on very restricted timetables, or undertake a block period of teaching for either 'recent and relevant' experience or research purposes. There is little evidence that student teachers on well organized and 'balanced' ITE courses, where there exist opportunities for significant proportions of supported school-based work, find their tutors 'lack' of recent teaching in schools a major issue. Most acknowledge the depth of experience that tutors have accrued resulting from a substantial period of teaching in schools before taking up posts in HEIs. Indeed an HE tutor's detachment from the school scene is often seen as a major benefit by the students who comment on the need for an independent and objective focus provided by the tutor, uncluttered by the pressures and politics of the school.

Back to First Principles — What's Wrong with 'Traditional' ITE?

McIntyre (1990b) argues that 'traditional' PGCEs have a number of weaknesses; namely that student teachers have marginal status in schools, that they are not in schools long enough to learn how to cope effectively with teaching or assimilate how schools 'work', that educational 'theorizing' is irrelevant to ITE, and that students have problems relating what tutors say in HEIs to what actually goes on in the classroom. He claims that there are few opportunities in schools to try out the advice given in the HEIs, that observation of teachers is limited and unstructured, and that visits by tutors are seen by students as 'judgmental assessments'. McIntyre also believes that students perform differently for different audiences and 'match' their performances to the perceived needs of the teacher or tutor who observes them (for example they see the HE tutor as a researcher, theoretician and largely concerned with 'good practice'). Worryingly he claims that 'most established patterns of teacher education appear to give student teachers the opportunity, which they generally accept, of avoiding the challenge of relating their educational thinking to their acquisition of teaching practices'.

Although there are elements of truth in all these assertions they can be countered with reference to research into students' perceptions of their ITE courses (Williams *et al.*, 1992). The structure of the HEI course experienced is clearly important. Those courses in which tutors encourage students to adopt enquiry-led, experiential and practical approaches and include 'well controlled and assessed guided study and experiment, rather than a didactic approach' (HMI, 1982) are favoured. Meighan and Harber (1986) also encourage the adoption of a democratic, power-sharing approach which both helps students cope with schools, and sees possible alternatives and modifications to their status quo.

It is revealing to bear in mind the findings of the OHMCI (1993c) concerning the new teacher in school. This survey, like its predecessors in 1981 and 1987, looked at how effectively initial training had equipped students for teaching in schools. Within it 94 per cent of heads in secondary schools felt that new teachers were adequately prepared for their first teaching post (85 per cent said 'well prepared'), with similarly high levels of satisfaction concerning professional competence, personal qualities, academic competence and commitment to teaching. In addition new teachers' knowledge of the National Curriculum was adjudged to be either 'good' or 'very good' by three-quarters of heads. (OHMCI, 1993c calculations on each of the factors listed above are slightly lower, although they state that 81 per cent of all new teachers are at least satisfactory.)

A Vision of the Future? The Articled and Licensed Teacher Schemes

The Articled Teacher Scheme might be considered as a foretaste of the changes towards more school-based work in ITE. The OHMCI (1993a) found most of these schemes to be generally satisfactory, producing competence in the new teacher at least parallel to that gained on a one-year PGCE. Many students also had a better appreciation of school life because of the two-year, school-based, nature of the scheme. However, there were some notable weaknesses where schools and teachers varied in the nature and quality of support they could provide. This emphasizes the continuing need for support from the teacher/mentor and HE tutor. The OHMCI report (1993a) focuses on the need for good partnership, sound mentor training and noted the difficulties mentors faced because of the increase in their responsibilities. This created time-management problems, for time was not available for mentors to plan their work effectively or take on additional tasks. There was also a concern that head teachers were selecting mentors on the grounds of 'staff development' rather than considerations of whether they were the best teachers to train students. This suggests that HE tutors still have an important role to play in the school-based training of students, a contention strengthened by the OHMCI (1993a) observation that 'What most mentors lacked was the necessary up to date and broad knowledge of current research and practice to enable them to provide articled teachers with a wide range of alternative approaches' (p. 15). This corresponds with evidence that HEIs sometimes had to repeat sections of ITE that were 'covered' in schools so as to ensure full student appreciation and understanding.

OHMCI (1993a) believe that 'regular visits from tutors were essential to ensure that the system of assessment was implemented rigorously' (p. 18) because the mentors who assessed teaching performance and marked students' written work sometimes had insufficient knowledge and experience to do so.

In their consideration of the Licensed Teacher Scheme OHMCI (1993b) found that training placements were adequate, but that only 15 per cent of these could be considered to be 'good'. Few schools provided well structured training and the problems of training mentors, gaining LEA support, and providing a range of educational experiences for students were acute. OHMCI (1993b) concluded that 'most licensed teachers need training in addition to that provided by their placement schools' (p. 10), again a clear indication of the need for an HE tutor's input.

This leads to the conclusion that any form of 'apprenticeship model' of ITE should be strongly resisted, because schools on their own find it difficult to make appropriate use of their expertise and have problems in helping students develop fully. Schools often provide a restricted range of knowledge and ideas relevant to practice in schools, and use idiosyncratic criteria for assessment which is at best heavily biased towards practicality and unlikely to develop the skills to rationally evaluate and develop teaching ability. A strong contribution from both school and HEI in partnership is therefore required.

Conclusion

In conclusion OHMCI (1993) clearly state that 'students gained most benefit when schools and college support were complementary' (4.35) and that 'It is necessary to establish, therefore, strong and effective partnerships between schools and HEIs, together with thorough monitoring and evaluation procedures' (p. 41). In the light of this need for partnerships to strengthen it is therefore extremely worrying that some universities are considering withdrawing entirely from ITE because of the financial pressures resulting from enforcing Circular 9/92 ('Universities set to abandon training' p. 2, *TES*, 16 July 1993).

The views of teachers involved in the training of students clearly illustrate the need for an HEI involvement. Back and Booth (1992) asked them what they thought the future roles of HEIs and tutors should be. The teachers were unanimous in their belief that both had a vitally important function and that 'ITT was not something that schools could undertake by themselves'. The roles identified for the HE tutor included arbitration between schools and HEIs, providing insight into theory and research, and being a focus for students of the same discipline to discuss and reflect upon practice.

Neither one agency nor the other can therefore successfully deliver their respective aspects of training without a workable, open, and honest partnership.

The HE tutor can be seen to have an important role in the training of new teachers and remains as a catalyst that strengthens the bond between different elements of the ITE system.

References

BACK, D. and BOOTH, M. (1992) 'Commitment to mentoring', in WILKIN, M. (Ed) *Mentoring in Schools*, London, Kogan Page.

BARRETT, E., BARTON, L., FURLONG, J., GALVIN, C., MILES, S. and WHITTY, G. (1993) *Initial Teacher Education in England and Wales: A Topography*, London, University of London Goldsmiths' College.

BEARDON, T., BOOTH, M., HARGREAVES, D. and REISS, M. (1992) *School-led Initial Teacher Training: The Way Forward*, Cambridge, Department of Education.

CATE (1992) *The Accreditation of Initial Teacher Training under Circulars 9/92 Department For Education and 35/92 (Welsh Office): A note of guidance from the Council for Accreditation of Teacher Education*, London, CATE.

DES/HMI (1991) *School-based Initial Teacher Training in England and Wales*, London, HMSO.

DFE (1992) *Initial Teacher Training (Secondary Phase) (Circular 9/92)*, London, HMSO.

EDWARDS, T. (1992) 'Issues and challenges in initial teacher education', *Cambridge Journal of Education*, 22, 3, pp. 283–91.

ELLIS, B. (1993) 'Training geography teachers: An increased role for schools', *Teaching Geography*, July.

FURLONG, V. J., HIRST, P. H., POCKLINGTON, K. and MILES, S. (1988) *Initial Teacher Training and the Role of the School*, Milton Keynes, Open University Press.

HARBER, C. and MEIGHAN, R. (1986a) 'A case study of democratic learning in education', *Educational Review*, 38, 3.

HMI (1982) *The New Teacher in School: A Report*, London, HMSO.

HMI (1983) *Teaching in Schools: The Content of Initial Training*, London, HMSO.

HMI (1987) *Quality in Schools: The Initial Training of Teachers*, London, HMSO.

HONES, G. (1992) 'Teacher education and classroom reality', in NAISH, M. (Ed) *Geography and Education*, London, Institute of Education, pp. 61–71.

JACQUES, K. (1992) 'Mentoring in initial teacher education', *Cambridge Journal of Education*, 22, 3, pp. 337–50.

KIRKHAM, D. (1992) 'The nature and conditions of good mentoring practice', in WILKIN, M. (Ed) *Mentoring in Schools*, London, Kogan Page, pp. 66–73.

LAWLOR, S. (1990) *Teacher Mistaught: Training in Theories or Education in Subjects*, London, Centre for Policy Studies.

MCINTYRE, D. (1990a) 'The Oxford Internship Scheme and the Cambridge analytical framework: Models of partnership in initial teacher education', in BOOTH, M., FURLONG, J. and WILKIN, M. *Partnership in Initial Teacher Training*, London, Cassell.

MCINTYRE, D. (1990b) 'Ideas and principles guiding the internship scheme', in BENTON, P. (Ed) *The Oxford Internship Scheme: Integration + Partnership in Initial Teacher Education*, London, Calouste Gulbenkian Foundation.

McManus, M. (1993) 'Oh yes, we can work together', *Times Educational Supplement*, 22 January, p. 16.

Meighan, R. and Harber, C. (1986) 'Democratic learning in teacher education: A review of experience at one institution', *Journal of Education for Teaching*, 12, 2.

O'Hear, A. (1988) *Who Teaches The Teachers?* London, Social Affairs Unit.

OHMCI (1993a) *The Articled Teacher Scheme: September 1990–July 1992*, London, HMSO.

OHMCI (1993b) *The Licensed Teacher Scheme: September 1990–July 1992*, London, HMSO.

OHMCI (1993c) *The New Teacher In School: A Survey by HM Inspectors in England and Wales 1992*, London, HMSO.

Smith, R. (1992) 'Theory: an entitlement to understanding', *Cambridge Journal of Education*, 22, 3, pp. 387–98.

Wilkin, M. (Ed) (1992a) *Mentoring in Schools*, London, Kogan Page.

Wilkin, M. (1992b) 'The challenge of diversity', *Cambridge Journal of Education*, 22, 3, pp. 307–22.

Williams, E. A., Butt, G. W. and Soares, A. (1992) 'Student perceptions of a secondary postgraduate certificate in education course', *Journal of Education for Teaching*, 17, 3, pp. 297–310.

Chapter 10

The Mentor

Anne Williams

A key development in initial teacher training at present is the transfer of responsibility for the support and training of students from higher education to school and from tutor to teacher. This chapter discusses some of the issues raised by this initiative for the teachers involved. It uses as illustration, information collected from teachers during the process of developing a secondary initial teacher-training course at the University of Birmingham which meets the requirements of Circular 9/92. The material used comes partly from a survey of heads of departments who were already working with students. This was intended to provide information for those designing workshops for mentors about the teachers' perceptions of their training needs. Other material is more anecdotal and is from discussions during course-development meetings much of which focused upon issues for the teachers who were to be given additional responsibilities.

Approaches to Mentoring

A clear picture of the mentoring process is needed if the task of the mentor is to be clarified and training or development needs identified. A number of dimensions to mentoring can be identified. These are represented in Figure 10.1, which attempts to present a framework for the analysis of mentoring activity. A range of the skills of mentoring and different levels at which mentoring can take place are included, as is an indication of the variety of contexts in which students may be expected to work. The first dimension is about contexts for mentoring which will vary, dependent upon the school culture and the agreed policies developed by schools and HEIs (Higher Education Institutions). They will also in part be created by the individual students placed in a school.

This dimension concerns the relative importance of subject-specific issues and wider professional concerns. It is also about whether particular issues are matters to be considered wholly or partially from

Figure 10.1: The Mentor Teacher

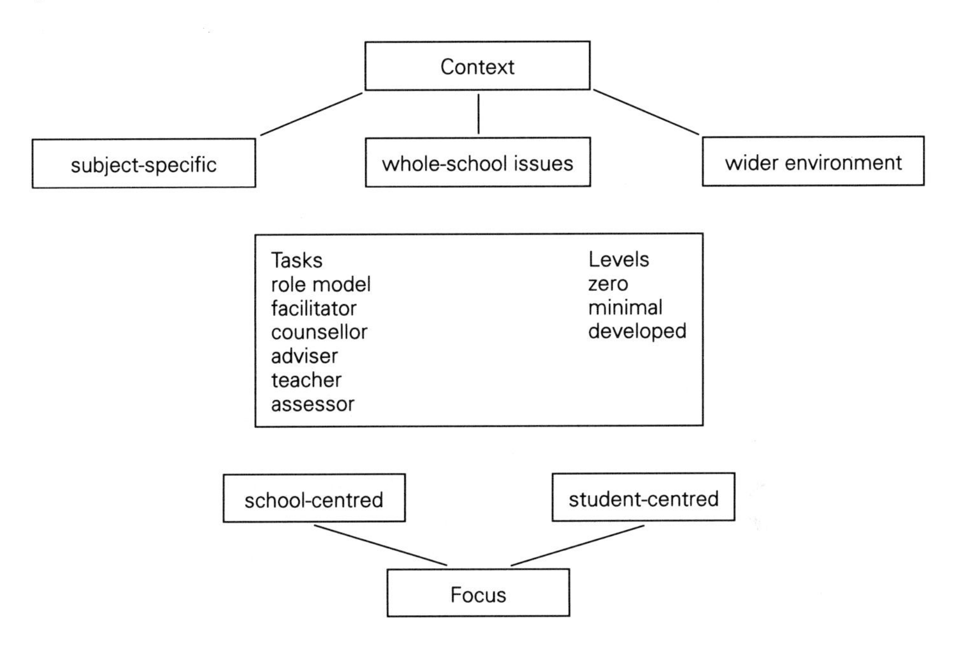

a subject point of view or with a more general, whole-school approach. Some approaches to improving mentoring practice, such as that developed in Cambridge (University of Cambridge Department of Education, 1990; Wilkin, 1992) place great emphasis upon the empowerment of teachers to undertake subject methods work with the student and make the effective teaching of a subject the main priority. This appears to be endorsed by the latest CATE criteria (DFE, 1992) although the criteria neither exclude a focus upon whole-school issues nor imply that a subject-specific focus with students necessarily demands a subject-specific approach to the development of mentoring skills. The criteria do nevertheless pay significantly less attention to what might be described as 'whole-school issues' than do those which preceded them (DES, 1984, 1989). The subject-based approach may be seen in practice from an examination of the mentor guidelines which arise from the Cambridge project (University of Cambridge Department of Education, op cit.). These, while developed in the context of supporting history students, are nevertheless of much wider application. For example, the headings of the guidelines include:

- Relationships with the Training Institution;
- Relationships with the Trainee;

- Induction and Planning a Programme for the Trainee, Observing the Trainee;
- Conducting a Debriefing Session (general procedures);
- Conducting a Debriefing Session (the subject-specific agenda); and
- The Wider Professional Role of the Trainee and the Assessment of the Trainee.

Clearly these headings would be applicable to student support in any subject area.

Other approaches lay greater emphasis upon a range of tasks and experiences to which the student teacher needs to be introduced, only part of which, albeit an important part, is concerned with subject teaching. The Oxford Internship Scheme (Benton, 1990), for example, involves the identification of a curriculum tutor (subject-specific) from the university and a mentor (subject-specific) from the school together with a general tutor from the university and a professional tutor from the school. In addition to the support and guidance which comes from the curriculum tutor and the mentor, weekly meetings are held between interns (students) and the school professional tutor addressing whole-school issues. This can of course be widened still further to incorporate links with parents, governors and the wider community.

Nolder, Smith and Melrose (1994) focus upon the personal factors and upon the importance of working together. They describe the mentor's role in terms of:

> supportive fellow professional;
> listening friend;
> supportive critic;
> gatekeeper and guide;
> link agent. (Jaworski and Watson, 1994, p. 42)

This is not to suggest that the above list is exhaustive, or that aspects of the mentor's role related to subject expertise are not important. It does, however, articulate one set of priorities if mentoring is to be successful and suggests that without these necessary personal attributes or skills, other parts of the mentor role including that related to subject-specific support are unlikely to be addressed successfully.

The second dimension concerns the focus of the mentoring activity itself. This can be placed on a continuum with the inculcation of a specific model of 'good practice' at one extreme which might be described as 'school-centred', and enabling the student to develop effective strategies at the other which could be described as 'student-centred'. The 'school-centred' approach emphasizes the importance of the student adopting the culture and practices of the school and of the teachers with whom he or she has contact. The mentor's role thus focuses upon inculcating the student into this culture and upon ensuring that strategies and procedures used in the school are adopted by the student. A student-centred model gives the mentor the task of analysing the individual needs of the beginning teacher so that programmes may be devised to meet their needs. Progress is monitored and training adapted accordingly. The priority is whether specific strategies and approaches are the best ones for the individual student's development as a teacher rather than whether they match practice in one school. Personal qualities such as the ability to evaluate performance critically, to be supportive when listening and so on are as important if not more important than subject expertise. It is an approach which may be found in schools receiving students undertaking conventional training and is often that adopted by the HEI tutor. Feedback from students on a conventional PGCE course (Williams *et al.*, 1992) suggests that one of the perceived benefits of the input from both school teachers and university tutors is that the latter are more student-centred in their approach whereas a common criticism of the advice offered within the school is that it reflects an individual school culture or policy excessively and takes insufficient account of the possibility of alternative strategies which might be more effective for an individual student. This of course raises important questions about the extent to which conflict can occur between the needs of the school and the needs of the student and how such potential conflict might be minimized.

Within the context of these two broad dimensions various mentoring activities can be identified. A wide range of roles for mentors have been identified by a number of writers, in the UK and elsewhere, in relation to supporting both students and newly qualified teachers. Wildman *et al.* (op cit.) talk about teachers, leaders, guides and role models in a variety of teaching contexts, and of the comprehensive range of strategies adopted by their sample in order to support beginning teachers. HMI describe the requirements of teachers whose role has changed from supervisor to teacher tutor as 'objective observation, assessment of competence levels in relation to agreed criteria, and provision of written and oral feedback on the student's preparation, teaching and evaluation of pupils' learning' (DES/HMI, 1991). Shaw (1992) describes good interpersonal skills, that is, the ability to encourage, empathize, listen, reflect, analyse, organize, be flexible and be approachable, as an essential prerequisite to effective mentoring. Hill, Jennings and

Madgewick (1992) categorize mentor competences in five ways: responsibility for establishing a supportive supervisory relationship; applying the counselling skills needed to become an effective helper; supporting the development of effective classroom practice; maintaining the beginning teacher's profile, monitoring and assessing work in the classroom; informing organizing and supporting other colleagues; identifying with colleagues appropriate specialisms within the school, other neighbouring schools and, where necessary, within an LEA cluster. Watkins (1992) identifies three major overlapping aspects of the mentor's role, namely, pastoral support to a new teacher, supervision and sequential introduction to professional issues in education. D'Arbon (1992) considers that the mentor oversees the immersion of the intern into the school culture in a number of ways, acts as a liaison between the school and the university, encourages engagement with the professional culture and acts as the focus person responsible for a particular intern in the school. Wilkin (1992) refers to differing conceptions of mentoring practice from mentoring as the development of subject presentation requiring training which will empower the teacher to undertake subject-based work with the student, to a needs' analysis model in which interpersonal skills are more important than subject expertise and in which the starting point is the student and his or her individual needs.

There is some evidence to support the importance of interpersonal skills in mentoring activity. For example Tellez (1992) suggests that, in the context of supporting the beginning teacher, the key to the success of any mentoring relationship is the willingness of the beginner to seek help which demands that he or she feels comfortable talking to the mentor. This is illustrated by a comment made by Lucy, a mathematics teacher (quoted in Jaworski and Watson, 1994).

> It's important to set up the right sort of relationship in the first place so that if you wander into the classroom, students don't feel intimidated and don't see you as checking up on them. It's how you set up the relationship which matters. You have to work with students. (Jaworski and Watson, 1994, p. 41)

Wildman *et al.* (1992) report that, in an analysis of 150 mentor–beginning-teacher relationships, the willingness of the experienced teacher to be a mentor was the most important characteristic in supporting and maintaining the relationship. This is particularly significant in the current circumstances in England and Wales where mentors may be taking on an increased role in student support because of government-imposed requirements rather than because the role is one which they felt they ought to play. Although resources are to be transferred to schools to support a more school-based approach to secondary teacher training, they are unlikely to be sufficient to recompense schools fully for the part they are to be asked to play. This is particularly so since the Secretary of State has said that schools are to be resourced for their additional rather than for their total commitments, and since the total level of resource available is significantly below that supporting the Articled Teacher Scheme which has demonstrated that school-based training is more expensive than conventional courses.

Elliott and Calderhead (1992) describe teachers' comments upon their role as mentors to students training through the Articled Teacher Scheme which involves students spending four-fifths of their time in school over a two-year full-time course of training. They note that while mentors describe their role in various ways, the mentor as someone who supports or nurtures the student is the most prevalent perception. Elliott and Calderhead note the relative absence of reference to the articulation of craft knowledge to the articled teacher and of reference to the mentor as challenging the student in order to develop learning and experience. They conclude that individual mentors appeared to adopt strategies which were compatible with their own perception of the mentor's role.

Within the different contexts and foci described, a number of strands or tasks can be identified. The first is the teacher as role model, that is a competent practitioner who can serve as an appropriate exemplar to a beginning teacher. The second requires the mentor to act as a facilitator in a variety of contexts. These may include introducing the student to other staff with specific expertise from which the student could learn or helping with access to resources. A third role may be that of counsellor, that is, someone with whom problems may be shared. There are also many instances where the mentor will be called upon to offer advice, for example, about teaching or management strategies or about communicating with other or senior staff or with parents. The mentor also acts as the student's teacher in some circumstances, perhaps through demonstrating a specific technique with a group of pupils or perhaps through observing and analysing the student's lessons. Finally, the mentor has a role as the assessor of the student's competence, a role which is not always easy to reconcile with that of counsellor and supporter.

A final perspective on mentoring derives from that provided by McIntyre and Hagger (1992) who put forward a number of views of mentoring which are increasingly ambitious in the expectations of those who are to fulfil the role, that is, different levels of mentoring. There is not space in this chapter to do justice to their concept of mentoring nor to offer a detailed critique and the brief résumé which follows may well oversimplify a complex analysis. It is nevertheless included in order to paint as complete a picture as possible of the many dimensions of mentoring and to indicate the meaning of the 'levels' of mentoring which are included in Figure 10.1. At one end of a continuum is what they describe as 'zero-level' mentoring in which teachers' expertise as teachers counts for nothing. This conception of mentoring, while not suggesting that teachers fail to offer support to students, sees the skills needed and used as those which can be drawn from models of mentoring in other contexts, frequently from the wider field of management including the management of induction and staff development. Thus, for example, a mentor's expertise in observing lessons and offering feedback could have been gained through training as an appraiser rather than through training specifically focused upon the needs of the student teacher.

'Minimal' mentoring involves the teacher on the basis of his or her expertise as a classroom teacher who is able to support and guide a student who is learning through practice. It is based on the premise that practising teachers are much better equipped than teacher educators to offer practical support to students. McIntyre and Hagger identify a number of tasks which need to be addressed by the supporting teacher such as ensuring that students are helped to develop planning skills as well as skills of classroom practice, or enabling students to recognize and learn from their strengths but also to face up to their problems. Distinctive strengths of school-based support are also identified such as the level of information which can be provided by a mentor by virtue of their in-depth knowledge of the school within which they work, or the level of continuity in supervision which may be provided because the mentor can be with the student on a day to day basis. This model draws upon the distinctive contribution which the mentor within the school can make and is thus far from making trivial demands of the mentor, but, it is argued, fails to take maximum advantage of teachers' expertise or of the school context within which they work.

'Developed mentoring' on the other hand makes effective use of the teacher's expertise in various strategies within the context of supporting the student teacher. Specifically identified are collaborative teaching, access to experienced teachers' craft knowledge, discussing learner-teachers' ideas and managing beginning teachers' learning opportunities. While suggesting that such a model of mentoring is necessary if justice is to be done to the complexity of the process of learning to teach, the writers acknowledge that it is only possible in a context of largely school-based teacher education with a classroom teacher as mentor as a key figure.

The strength of the model presented in Figure 10.1 is that it can be applied to many different patterns of mentoring practice, since the relative importance of the different context, roles and activities are not specified. A very minimal mentor programme meeting only the most basic interpretation of the guidance given by CATE (CATE, 1992) can be understood within its parameters as can a very comprehensive and thoroughly tried and tested scheme.

The Starting Point

Teachers have been involved with the training of students for many years, although the role has rarely been clearly or formally defined. If training is to be provided for teachers undertaking a changing and evolving role, then it seems sensible to ask for their views of current strengths and weaknesses and of the sorts of training which might be needed. This was done at Birmingham in Autumn 1993 by means of a questionnaire to all teachers who had worked with students during that term. Details of responses are described in more detail in Williams (1993).

Asked to identify what they saw as their strengths as prospective mentors, the comments made by different respondents indicate a range of perceptions which could be placed upon the 'subject-specific'–'wider professional issues' continuum. There appears to be a number of respondents who see their current strengths largely in terms of their experience of teaching a particular subject and, in some cases, in terms of an ability to advise others about a wide range of subject-specific strategies: 'Experience as a successful class teacher.' Others were more specific, referring to breadth of knowledge: 'In depth knowledge of all aspects of the subject and teaching methods.' Others made reference to the need to be able to pass this knowledge on to others: 'Being able to advise on a wide range of techniques in teaching geography.'

It is also clear that for a number of respondents, their perceived strengths as mentors lie in the breadth of their experience over and above their responsibilities as subject teachers: 'The ability to offer a wide variety of advice in many areas of school life, not just my subject.' 'The ability to be helpful and informative about not only my subject but also extra-curricular activities and general affairs.'

If Elliott and Calderhead's conclusion that mentors will adopt strategies compatible with their own perceptions of the mentor's role is accepted, then the different views of mentor strengths articulated by this group of teachers have implications for the structures adopted in order to ensure that appropriate support is available to students.

The importance of interpersonal skills identified earlier (Tellez, op. cit., Wildman *et al.*, op. cit.) is endorsed by a number of this sample in the comments made about mentor strengths. Some of these were both about specific skills such as communication or listening.

> I hope I'm positive and approachable and a good listener;
> Ability to communicate to students;
> An empathy with the student;
> A sympathetic and constructive approach.

Others talked about the importance of wanting to work with students.

> An interest in assisting those interested in joining the profession;
> I want to be involved in PGCE training;
> Many students in the department in the past have completed practices in my care.

It would be interesting to know whether absence of comment about these areas reflected a belief that they were not important or simply indicated relative priorities. Although this survey did not address questions about school or student-centred approaches, it might be concluded, albeit tentatively, that respondents stressing interpersonal skills or an interest in work with students might adopt a more student-centred approach to mentoring. Equally tentatively, it could be suggested that those who see strengths in terms of subject teaching might adopt a more school-centred approach although the relationship here seems much more tenuous.

Asked to identify weaknesses, two responses dominated — lack of time and lack of information.

> A poor knowledge of the rest of the student teacher's course and expectations;
> Lack of detailed knowledge of present *modus operandi.* of schools of education in preparing students for teaching practice;
> Trying to find sufficient time to provide assistance for student;
> Severe lack of time.

Given the predominance of these two responses, it was not surprising to find that, when invited to specify particular areas where they felt that training was needed, many respondents requested information and the opportunity to discuss the course with university tutors and with other teachers.

> More awareness of the content of the PGCE course;
> The general framework of the new supervisory role, the legal requirements in particular full information on what is required.

When asked about perceived capability with reference to a range of specific mentoring tasks, it is not surprising to find that most teachers felt competent to undertake tasks which were largely organizational or which involved them in a facilitating role. Many of these are areas where expertise/experience from a different context may be applied to student support. For example, helping with resources or with meeting other staff would be needed for all new staff or newly qualified teachers as well as for students. It is interesting that while many teachers feel competent to discuss a lesson in advance, to observe it and to discuss it afterwards, far fewer feel confident in giving written feedback. At an anecdotal level this reflects a discussion which took place some time ago between representatives from a large number of teaching-practice schools, and university tutors. Teachers attached very significantly less importance to giving written feedback to students than did the university tutors or, more important, the students themselves who saw written feedback as essential.

Generally the numbers of teachers who identify a need for training in areas which might be described as specific to the initial teacher-training context, for example, helping students to set targets, assessing their overall performance or providing written feedback on lessons, does suggest a commitment to a level of mentoring which goes beyond the 'zero' level mentioned earlier.

It seems clear that it should not be assumed that teachers in schools lack skills which are possessed by tutors in universities and which need to be passed on. The time pressures mentioned by many respondents together with the other demands upon their time in school mean that the nature of mentoring activity when undertaken by a teacher who is in the school full-time will necessarily differ from that activity as undertaken by a visiting tutor. The part played hitherto, for example, by the university tutor as facilitator, is not necessarily very comparable with the role which will be played by the mentor undertaking the same task. The most effective way of providing feedback upon lessons observed by a tutor visiting a school may not be the most effective way of working for a subject teacher who is in the school full-time with a range of other responsibilities.

Early Impressions

Our partnership scheme is in its infancy, but already a number of issues are emerging for mentors. The first is a growing recognition for many mentors that mentoring is a whole-school or whole-department issue rather than a task to be given to a single individual. Most partnership schemes identify one person in the school as the mentor or one person in each subject department. Costings for transfer of funds are often based upon release of time for meetings between mentor and student. Within the partnership scheme developed at Birmingham, schools have used the funding transferred to them in different ways, including supporting the work undertaken with students within subject departments. It has been interesting to note that, in most cases where there has been consultation within the school, staff have chosen to retain money within the department for its shared use, rather than making a payment to one named member of staff. This seems to represent a recognition by many mentors that student support involves everyone and is not best undertaken by a single individual to the exclusion of other staff. As one individual commented, the allocation of funding to him to pay for weekly meetings had caused considerable departmental friction because other staff felt, rightly in his view, that they contributed just as importantly to the student's development as a teacher. He had decided to share the money which he received with other members of his department. Others are known to have made similar decisions.

Perhaps one of the commonest perceived role conflicts is between that of counsellor/supporter and that of assessor. As one teacher put it during a discussion of issues which were arising during the first year of mentor support for students,

> We used to be the ones who picked them up and put them back on their feet after you'd been in, but now we are the ones who have to give them the bad news as well as the good.

It is difficult to assess the extent to which this is or should be a problem. Certainly tutors were quick to point out in response to the above comment, that equally often they had to pick the student up after a bad experience in school and that past feedback from a number of students suggested that surviving school practice at all would have been problematic without the support of the tutor. There is, nevertheless, some evidence from teachers involved with Articled Teacher Schemes (Hill, Jennings and Madgewick in Wilkin, 1992) that the supportive mentor finds it not only difficult to change to an assessor, but also that he or she tends to feel that student failure will reflect failure on his or her part and thus be reluctant to make such a judgment. The sharing of responsibility and the sharing of problems and successes within the department may offer a mechanism for the support of a mentor who finds the role of assessor and, possibly, bearer of bad news, a difficult one to undertake. The sharing of these with the school's senior management seems equally important.

Many mentors have been surprised at how demanding their role has been and admit they have underestimated the amount of support which students have received, in the past, from the visiting tutor. Ironically, as one commented, the better they do the job, the more demanding it becomes as students gain confidence in them and feel able to bring problems and questions to them. This reinforces findings with respect to the Articled Teacher Scheme, in which, despite more generous resourcing than is now available for initial teacher-training courses, teachers felt that they did not have sufficient time to discharge fully their role as mentor. It raises questions of how much can reasonably be expected of teachers who still have to fulfil a role as a teacher of children, and, if choices have to be made, what priorities should be identified for the mentor.

A further issue which is evolving is that of a change of emphasis from enabling students to practise teaching, with some feedback on how this is progressing, to one in which practising teaching is a part of a school placement, but giving opportunities for students to learn while in a classroom is another important part of a mentor's role. Much early discussion during workshops for mentors centred upon the acceptability, or otherwise of 'interrupting' a student who was teaching a lesson. For many mentors this was seen initially as unacceptable and undermining to the student whose 'practice' was being subjected to unwarranted interference. Their view of their role was of an informed observer rather than as someone who could or should play an active role in the lesson. On further reflection, and following opportunities to work with students, this view has been replaced, for many, with one which sees teacher and student or two students working collaboratively as a powerful means of learning for the student, while at the same time enhancing the learning of pupils. A physical-education mentor commented,

> I am beginning to see how much potential there is in working together with the student rather than simply observing her teaching. By sharing dance-teaching lessons for half a term, she has gained confidence in leading some parts while learning

> from watching me introduce or develop aspects of which she is unsure. The pupils have gained because there will always be two of us going round to help them.

From the perspective of the beginning teacher, a mathematics NQT reinforces the possibility of learning from a mentor during the course of a lesson rather than always waiting for feedback subsequently.

> I don't like it when people observe you and sit at the back writing all the time. I would much prefer it if part-way through they come and talk with you about how things are going, perhaps throw a few ideas around . . . (quoted in Jaworski and Watson, 1994, p. 48)

This echoes comments made in the course of conversation with students, who rightly went on to emphasize the importance of prior planning for any form of collaborative working. This applies whether it refers to agreeing with the student that it is all right to engage him or her in conversation during the course of the lesson or whether it involves a planned joint lesson as in the examples below.

As a Year 9 English class was facing new curriculum and assessment requirements, it was agreed that Catherine would team teach a group with the head of department. Teaching Shakespeare to this age group was fairly new in the school but the head of department was keen to try and Catherine had looked at practical approaches to Shakespeare on the PGCE course. The head of department and Catherine worked together to plan a unit of work, with lead lessons which were taught on an alternate basis. The 'observer' focused on the pupils' reactions to a range of new approaches and these were discussed at the end of each session. At the end of the unit, the head of department put on a departmental workshop on 'practical approaches to Shakespeare' to which Catherine made a significant contribution.

Martin had been finding it difficult to plan for differentiated work with a mixed-ability Year 9 science group, mainly because he was worried about possible safety problems if he didn't get it quite right first go. He discussed this with the class teacher and they agreed that he would plan for four different activities and take responsibility for organizing the class, after which the teacher would take responsibility for two of the activities while he looked after the other two. Martin would then lead a whole-class discussion/summary at the end of the lesson and also be responsible for the timing of the lesson. In subsequent weeks he took over responsibility for three of the four activities and finally for the whole class with the teacher simply observing.

Benefits of Being a Mentor

Many general comments have been made about students bringing benefits to schools as well as making demands upon them. It is appropriate in this chapter to note a number of staff-development issues which mentors have identified.

The first is the value of rethinking one's own approach to teaching which has been fostered in general mentor-training sessions, which are undertaken in mixed subject groups. In analysing mentor-course evaluations, this is one feature which recurs.

> It makes you look at your own teaching again which is no bad idea;
> Some of it has inspired me with new ideas for my own teaching.

This process of revisiting one's own practice is enhanced by the fact that mentor courses have included teachers from different subject areas and also from different schools and different LEAs. For a significant proportion of mentors this has been their first opportunity for some time to have a professional discussion outside the context of their own school.

There has also been at least one example of a mentor identified by a deputy head as rethinking his approach to specific aspects of his teaching as a result of working with the student, although he had not thought that this was a particularly significant feature of his mentor training. For the deputy head, responsible for staff development within the school, this was a clearly identifiable bonus.

A number of mentors are also rethinking their attitudes to collaborative teaching as a result of discussing this with other mentors and trying it out, with tutor support and encouragement, with students. There is a growing recognition, not only of the potential of this practice for enhancing student learning, but also of the potential benefits for pupils of having, effectively, more than one teacher in the room. Allied to this is a changing attitude towards students working in pairs. A number of mentors who have previously felt that the only 'real' experience was standing up alone in front of a class have commented upon their changed perceptions of student pairings.

In some schools, students have worked in large groups at an early stage in their training. This can bring great benefits to all parties involved. Students work with small groups of pupils and are able to focus at an early stage on pupil learning rather than being overwhelmed by management issues. Pupils reap the benefits of individual attention and a ready source of help should they need it.

For senior staff who are involved in planning and teaching aspects of whole-school issues, such as pastoral care, reporting achievement to parents or dealing with disruptive pupils, there can be mutual benefits from sharing good practice and access to particular schools' expertise. For example, in planning a session which looked at raising student awareness of the need to involve senior staff or outside agencies with specific pupils problems, one school's counsellor offered to provide case-study material which was then used by other participating schools and which is now available for other workshops, possibly with NQTs in those schools.

Conclusion

The different patterns of mentoring practice, which were identified in relation to the model presented earlier in this chapter seem to be emerging in practice as our partnership course develops. Mentors clearly varied in their perceptions of their future role when first asked about the training needs. Their views on the challenges which have faced them so far and on the benefits which involvement as mentors has brought also vary. The extent to which mentors have interpreted their role within the confines of their subject or extended their role to a much broader consideration of the student as a developing teacher has varied reflecting each mentors' belief in the relative importance of subject-specific issues and whole-school concerns.

The fact that many have revisited their own teaching indicates an interest in assessing student strategies on merit rather than in relation to a preconceived notion of what constitutes good practice. Others have admitted to finding this difficult to achieve. The diversity of the mentor role has come as a surprise to some. Most have welcomed it, while concerned about the lack of time to do justice to the job, while others will not remain in the partnership in the future, having decided that they have other priorities. There is clearly a challenge to all partners in initial teacher training to develop mentor expertise in ways which acknowledge the different strengths and abilities which individual teachers can bring to their role as mentor but which also offer students basic entitlements and a sufficient consistency of experience. The comments made by the mentors quoted in this chapter, both prior to entering into partnership arrangements and during the first year of partnership operation, support the view that the development of the mentoring role and of expertise is a long-term undertaking and that highly sophisticated processes of mentor support cannot be created overnight. As Jaworski and Watson note,

> New mentors may be concerned with knowing the course, time-tabling the students, keeping their own teaching going, establishing contact with the HEI, and so on. (Jaworski and Watson, 1994, p. 124)

It is only after these concerns have been resolved that further development will take place.

References

Benton, P. (1990) *The Oxford Internship Scheme*, London, Calouste Gulbenkian Foundation.

CATE (1992) *The Accreditation of Initial Teacher Training Under Circulars 9/92 (Department For Education) and 35/92 (Welsh Office). A note of guidance from the Council for the Accreditation of Teachers*, London, CATE.

D'Arbon, T. (1992) 'Seeking a comparative perspective: A case study from Australia', in McIntyre, D., Hagger, H. and Wilkin, M. (1992) *Mentoring: Perspectives on School-Based Teacher Education*, London, Kogan Page.

DES (1984) *Initial Teacher Training: Approval of Courses (Circular 3/84)*, London, HMSO.

DES (1989) *Initial Teacher Training: Approval of Courses (Circular 24/89)*, London, HMSO.

DES/HMI (1991) *School-based Initial Teacher Training in England and Wales*, London, HMSO.

DFE (1992) *Initial Teacher Training (Secondary Phase) (Circular 9/92)*, London, HMSO.

Elliott, B. and Calderhead, J. (1992) 'Mentoring for teacher development: Possibilities and Caveats', in McIntyre, D., Hagger, H. and Wilkin, M. (1992) *Mentoring: Perspectives on School-based Teacher Education*, London, Kogan Page.

Hill, A., Jennings, M. and Madgewick, B. (1992) 'Initiating a Mentorship Training Programme', in Wilkin, M. (Ed) (1992) *Mentoring in Schools*, London, Kogan Page.

Jaworski, B. and Watson, A. (1994) *Mentoring in Mathematics Teaching*, London, Falmer Press.

McIntyre, D. and Hagger, H. (1992) 'Teachers' Expertise and Models of Mentoring', in McIntyre, D., Hagger, H. and Wilkin, M. (1992) *Mentoring: Perspectives on School-based Teacher Education*, London, Kogan Page.

NOLDER, R., SMITH, S. and MELROSE, J. (1994) 'Working together: Roles and Relationships in the Mentoring Process', in JAWORSKI, B. and WATSON, A. (1994) *Mentoring in Mathematics Teaching*, London, Falmer Press.

OHMCI (1993a) *The Articled Teacher Scheme: September 1990–July 1992*, London, HMSO.

OHMCI (1993b) *The Licensed Teacher Scheme: September 1990–July 1992*, London, HMSO.

SHAW, R. (1992) *Teacher Training in Secondary Schools*, London, Kogan Page.

TELLEZ, K. (1992) 'Mentors by choice not design: help-seeking by beginning teachers', in *Journal of Teacher Education*, 43, 3, pp. 214–21.

UNIVERSITY OF CAMBRIDGE DEPARTMENT OF EDUCATION (1990) *Guidelines for Mentors and Supervisors*, Cambridge.

WATKINS, C. (1992) 'An experiment in mentor training', in WILKIN, M. (Ed) (1992) *Mentoring in Schools*, London, Kogan Page.

WILDMAN, T.M., MAGLIARO, S.G., NILES, R.A. and NILES, J.A. (1992) 'Teacher mentoring: An analysis of roles, activities and conditions', in *Journal of Teacher Education*, 43, 3, pp. 205–13.

WILKIN, M. (Ed) (1992) *Mentoring in Schools*, London, Kogan Page.

WILLIAMS, E.A. (1993) 'Teacher perceptions of their needs as mentors in the context of developing school-based initial teacher education', in *British Educational Research Journal*, 19, 4, pp. 407–20.

WILLIAMS, E.A., BUTT, G. and SOARES, A. (1992) 'Student perceptions of a secondary postgraduate certificate in education course', in *Journal of Education of Teaching*, 18, 3, pp. 297–309.

Appendix 1

Professional Competences of the Successful Teacher

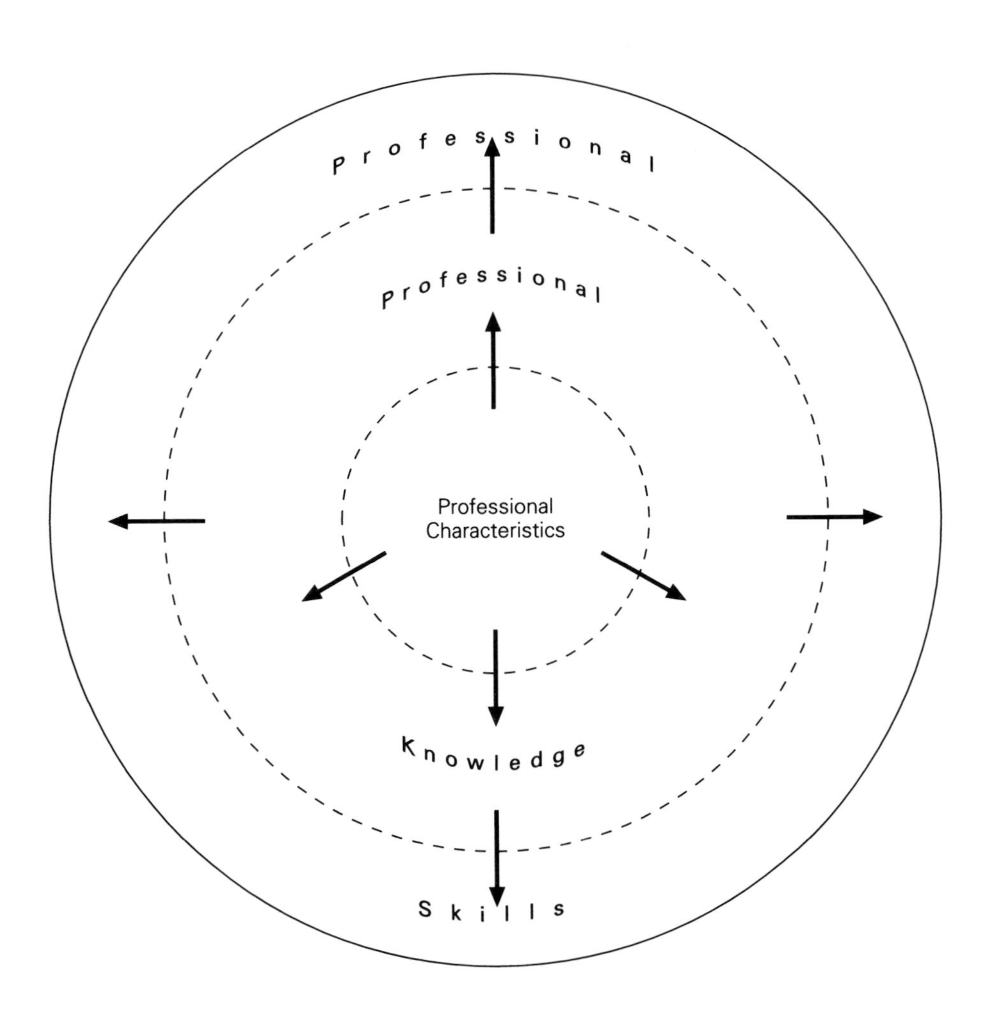

COMPETENCES		SCHOOL EXP	PHASE
1.4.5	awareness of contemporary debates about education;	2	Ac
1.4.6	understanding of schools as institutions and their place within the community;	1	Ac
1.4.7	knowledge of the part of the education system in which he or she is working and its relationship to other parts of that system;	1	aB
1.4.8	knowledge of the organisation and management of schools, and the place within these of school policies and development plans.	3	aBc
1.5	Knowledge of the teacher's role		
	Demonstrates:		
1.5.1	awareness of the importance of informed critical reflection in evaluating his or her professional practice;	2	Abc
1.5.2	understanding of how to draw upon sources of professional help and expertise;	3	aB
1.5.3	knowledge of his or her contractual, legal pastoral and administrative responsibilities;	2	aBc
1.5.4	awareness of his or her role as a member of a professional team within the school;	5	abC
1.5.5	awareness of how to respond to current social problems which may manifest themselves in schools.	2	aC

2	PROFESSIONAL SKILLS		
2.1	Subject application		
2.1.1	Plans appropriate lessons within teaching programmes.	3	Ab
2.1.2	Demonstrates a knowledge of the particular methodologies and procedures necessary for effective teaching of the subject(s) forming the content of his or her teaching.	3	Ab
2.1.3	Is able to prepare appropriate learning materials for pupils.	3	Ab

Appendix 2

Partnership PGCE

1 Principles Within the Partnership PGCE

Goldsmiths College remains committed to:

- equal opportunities;
- active and participative models of teaching and learning;
- the development of reflective practice; and
- the promotion of a broadly based and relevant curriculum for all children.

Senior management in schools remain committed to:

- involvement in training new teachers as part of the school's overall plan for the professional development of staff;
- the support of school-based tutors by ensuring that release time is available to work with students and attend meetings;
- the coordination of cross-curricular work sited in school; and
- the principles espoused by Goldsmiths.

School and college-based tutors remain committed to:

- maintaining good working relationships;
- good practice and curriculum development within the subject area;
- the education and professional support of students and newly qualified teachers; and
- the principles espoused by Goldsmiths.

2 Principles of Partnership PGCE Mentor Training 1992–3

1 'Mentor training' is not a 'one-off' exercise but an ongoing process of professional development.
2 The focus and processes involved will to some extent, be dependant upon factors such as:

(i) The stage of the partnership.
(ii) The previous experience of school-based tutors.
Thus at any one time, the training will need to be closely geared to the particular needs of school-based tutors.

3 'Mentor training' should not be conceived as a one way process in which college tutors train the teachers to train the students but rather as a reciprocal process in which both sides have much to learn.
4 'Mentor training' should operate within agreed educational principles (see Appendix 2.1).
5 Teacher education takes place in different contexts and sites which are complementary. Each has a unique contribution to make to the process which will be refined through:
   (i) Formal 'training' sessions.
   (ii) The operation of and reflection upon what is involved in partnership work which includes:
   *selection of students
   *planning of courses
   *teaching students in school and college
   *assessing students learning
   *monitoring and evaluating the partnership
   (iii) The exchange and dissemination of ideas between school and college-based tutors. This includes circulation of papers written by tutors and curriculum development projects undertaken by students.
6 Formal 'training' sessions should address a number of strands:
   (i) The content, structure and implementation of the course over the year.
   (ii) Key areas of the supervision process e.g.: advice and support; classroom observation; target setting; giving feedback; pastoral care.
   (iii) Curriculum development initiatives within school and college.
   (iv) The monitoring and evaluation of partnerships.
7 Whilst (i), (iii) and (iv) will be largely subject-specific, there are obvious possibilities for common sessions for (ii).
8 Monitoring and evaluation will be achieved through:
   (i) Provision of agendas and minutes for all 'training' sessions.
   (ii) Provision of common evaluation proforma to all school-based tutors.
   (iii) Ongoing discussion of partnership with respect to the aims of the course including the quality of training offered to students.
   (iv) Cross-subject evaluation meetings.

Notes on Contributors

Richard Aplin taught French in comprehensive schools in Wiltshire and Oxfordshire for 16 years before taking up posts in teacher education. From 1985 to 1986 he taught at University College of Swansea and was a member of the Oxford Internship Development Group from 1986 to 1987. He is currently Modern Languages Tutor and Head of Secondary PGCE at the University of Leicester. He has written and co-written a number of language course materials published by Hodder and Stoughton or broadcast by the BBC. He is the bibliography editor for the international journal Language Awareness and is the author of *A Dictionary of Contemporary France* (Hodder and Stoughton, 1993).

Graham Butt is a Lecturer in Education and Geography Methods Tutor within the School of Education, The University of Birmingham. He is a member of the Geographical Association and is the Chair of its Examination and Assessment Group. His research and writing focuses mainly on aspects of teaching and examining in geography.

Sally Inman is currently Tutor for Professional Development in the Department of Educational Studies at Goldsmiths College, London. She is also the Director of the Centre for Cross Curricular Initiatives. Sally has been involved in school based teacher education for many years and, with Mary Stiasny, pioneered the Goldsmiths PGCE Secondary partnership scheme.

Peter Lucas has had wide experience of teaching at a variety of levels, including secondary schools. He is a member of the Teacher Professional Development Research Group in the Division of Education, University of Sheffield. He recently retired as a senior lecturer in the Division of Education and tutor in charge of the PGCE history course to concentrate on research. A former director of the University of Sheffield secondary PGCE programme, his involvement with such programmes continues in the new 'partnership' era as a chief examiner for a Midlands university and as a member of the monitoring and evaluation group for a northern university. He has published papers on a range of professional development topics including several on the nature and practice of supervision.

Pat Mahony has worked in the area of Teacher Education for the last twenty years. She is currently Head of the Department of Educational Studies, Faculty of Education, Goldsmiths College University of London. She has written extensively in the area of Equal Opportunities and more recently on teacher competences.

Anna Pendry is a Lecturer in the University of Oxford Department of Educational Studies. She is currently the Tutor for the PGCE Course, and also teaches at both PGCE and advanced degree level in relation to history education. Her research interests include aspects of teacher education and specifically beginner teachers' learning.

Susan Sidgewick is a Lecturer in the Department of Educational Studies at Goldsmiths College where she teaches on the secondary PGCE programme and manages the department's courses for newly qualified teachers. She is coordinator of the steering group overseeing development of the PGCE in partnership with secondary schools, and is researching and writing in the area of policy in relation to teacher education.

Mary Stiasny is a Lecturer in Education at Goldsmiths College. She is currently Head of Programme for PGCE Secondary and, with Sally Inman, she pioneered the original Social Studies partnership course, which the whole programme has now adopted. She is Director of the Centre for Education, Training and the local Economic Community at Goldsmiths, and has directed several EATE/TPS projects at the college.

Geoff Whitty is the Karl Mannheim Professor of Sociology of Education and Chair of the Department of Policy Studies at the Institute of Education, University of London. He was formerly Professor and Dean of Education at Bristol Polytechnic and the Goldsmiths' Professor of Policy and Management in Education at Goldsmiths College, University of London. He chaired a Working Party on Competence-based Teacher Education for the Council for National Academic Awards and a Working Group on Competences in Teacher Education for the Department of Education in Northern Ireland. He is currently co-director of the ESRC-funded Modes of Teacher Education (MOTE) research project.

Anne Williams is a Senior Lecturer at the University of Birmingham and is Senior Tutor for PGCE Courses. She has been responsible for the development of the secondary partnership course at Birmingham and also teaches at PGCE and higher degree level in physical education. She has published extensively in the area of physical education and is currently researching and writing about secondary initial teacher education.

Barbara Wynn is the Headteacher of The Willink School in Berkshire which is involved in a partnership with Reading University for the training of new teachers. She was formerly Deputy Head of Cheney Upper School in Oxford and Senior Teacher at Didcot Girls' School: in both these posts she was actively involved in the setting up and development of the Internship Scheme with Oxford University. In addition she served as the first teacher examiner for the PGCE course at Oxford University from 1991 to 1993. She is also a governor of Oxford Brookes University.

Index